D1624515

THE AUTHOR OF THE *PROMETHEUS BOUND*

THE NEW DELPHIN SERIES

PUBLISHED IN ASSOCIATION WITH
Arion: A Journal of Humanities and the Classics

THE AUTHOR OF THE
PROMETHEUS BOUND

BY C. J. HERINGTON

UNIVERSITY OF TEXAS PRESS
AUSTIN AND LONDON

International Standard Book Number 0–292–70044–X
Library of Congress Catalog Card Number 75–132528
© 1970 by C. J. Herington
All Rights Reserved
Printed by The University of Texas Printing Division, Austin
Bound by Universal Bookbindery, Inc., San Antonio

PREFACE

The original version of this work was composed for a seminar on ancient tragedy held during the American Philological Association's meeting in Toronto in December of 1968. I take pleasure in thanking my friends Professors Desmond Conacher and Leon Golden, who organized the seminar and invited me to contribute; the trustees of the Guggenheim Foundation, who have afforded me the leisure to study this and other aspects of the *Prometheus*; and Miss Sunya Anderson, who has twice typed a difficult draft with great skill and patience.

During the last two generations such able scholars as Porzig, Schmid, Lesky, Friedrich, and Else have expressed —in varying tones and pitches—doubts about the authenticity of the *Prometheus Bound*. My own enquiries early convinced me that they were well justified. By comparison with the other plays of Aeschylus, and even with the rest of the surviving tragic corpus, the *Prometheus* is a highly eccentric play, from its grand structure down to the smallest details of phrasing and meter. Prima facie, therefore, the opponents of its authenticity have a perfectly serious case, one that cannot properly be dismissed (as so often it is, especially among English-speaking scholars) in the princely manner of a D. H. Lawrence—with a thump on the chest and a resounding "I feel it HERE!"

In writing this monograph I had three principal aims. First, to restate the conditions of the problem, as they appeared after the down-dating of the *Supplices*. Second, to catalogue what seemed to be the relevant phenomena: the actual or supposed eccentricities of the play. Lastly, to frame a hypothesis that would account for as many of those phenomena as possible. During and after the meeting at Toronto many colleagues, notably Professors Seth Benardete and Herbert Musurillo, offered generous advice and criticism, to the great benefit of the present version. Even now it does not pretend to completeness, being intended as a contribution to informed debate rather than as a definitive statement. How many lines of investigation remain open is shown, for example, by A. F. Garvie's *Aeschylus' "Supplices": Play and Trilogy* (Cambridge, 1969), which reached me just as my typescript was about to go to press. I take this opportunity to refer to its very thorough discussion of the papyrus hypothesis of a play from the *Supplices* trilogy, and to the statistics on Aeschylean usage at pages 83 and 124; all of which seem to reinforce the conclusions drawn in the present study.

The names of the extant plays of Aeschylus are abbreviated thus: *PV* for *Prometheus Vinctus*; otherwise as Italie's

Index Aeschyleus. For the line numbers of the plays I refer to the second edition of the Oxford text by Gilbert Murray (1955). I cite the fragments most often from Mette's *Die Fragmente der Tragödien des Aischylos* (abbreviated to M; e.g., "Fr. 300 M") but occasionally also from Nauck's *Tragicorum Graecorum Fragmenta* (e.g., "Fr. 219 N").

November 1969   C. J. H.
Austin, Texas

CONTENTS

THE AUTHOR OF THE *PROMETHEUS BOUND*

CHAPTER I

General Considerations: Criteria

After reviewing, often with admiration, much of the literature that has been devoted to the authorship of the *Prometheus* over the past century,[1] I feel no doubt whatever as
to where to begin. When a man denies that Poem *A* is
rightly attributed to Poet *X*, exactly what is he doing? To
my mind, there are two main answers:

1. He is rejecting such external testimony as may exist to
the effect that Poem *A* is Poet *X*'s work. Where the *Prometheus* is concerned, this means that he is rejecting the judgment of the Alexandrian scholars. For the Alexandrians cer-

---

[1] For accounts of the origin and progress of the controversy, see
Schmid (I) pp. 1–5 and Coman pp. 5–8.

tainly catalogued and commented on the play as the un-
doubted work of Aeschylus.[2] The *Catalogue* preserved in
codd. MV, and the earlier strata of the *Prometheus* scholia,
are sufficient proof of this. The Medicean scholia not only
assume throughout that Aeschylus is the author but also
appeal (as the Alexandrian scholars regularly did) to his
συνήθεια, his poetic practice, here as in their comments on
the other plays.[3] Some, at least, of the men who originally
wrote these notes had an eye for general poetic character as
well as for lexicographical detail; and we must not forget
the vast extent of the comparative material on which they
could and—even on the mutilated evidence of the scholia
—did in fact draw. Among many other lost works, they
could consult the *Unbound* (scholia on *PV* 511, 522) and
the *Pyrphoros* (on *PV* 94). Furthermore, the Hellenistic
scholars who edited Attic drama were, on the whole, as much
alert to the possibility of misattribution as were any of their
nineteenth-century German successors; and when in doubt
they could refer not only to the dramas that are now lost,
but also to the complete *Didascaliae*. The tradition has, in
fact, preserved a remarkably full record of their views on

[2] Schmid himself admitted this in (II), col. 222. For a list of the
ancient testimonia to the *Prometheus Bound*'s authorship, see ibid.,
n. 8. They are printed in full by Coman, Chapter I; his discussion,
however, contains some strange mistakes, in view of which his
numbers 4 and 5 should be removed from the list.

[3] M-scholia on *PV* 256, 707; cf. those on 177 and 355, where the
lines concerned are said to be characteristic of Aeschylus' μεγαλοφυΐα
and φύσις, respectively.

the authenticity of the dramatic corpus.[4] Most instructive as to their methods and criteria is the First Hypothesis to the *Rhesus*—the only other extant Attic tragedy, apart from the *PV*, whose authenticity has been seriously disputed in modern times. Here we read of ancient scholars who were not in the least deterred, even by the existence of superficially firm documentary evidence for Euripidean authorship in the *Didascaliae*, from arguing about the authenticity of the text that lay before them. The *Rhesus* displayed the Σοφόκλειον χαρακτῆρα, maintained some; no, retorted others, at any rate ἡ περὶ τὰ μετάρσια ἐν αὐτῷ πολυπραγμοσύνη τὸν Εὐριπίδην ὁμολογεῖ!

I do not say that all ancient scholars were infallible—one side or the other must have been wrong in the debate over the *Rhesus*[5]—but I do wish to emphasize the following points:

[4] The ancient *Vitae* of Sophocles, Euripides, and Aristophanes each contain a note on the number of plays that were adjudged spurious in their respective author's corpus. The first cites Aristophanes of Byzantium as its authority; the second and third specify the plays concerned by name. The anonymous tract *De Comoedia* in Kaibel, pp. 6–10, carefully records the number of spurious, as well as of genuine, comedies that circulated under the names of Epicharmus, Magnes, and Aristophanes. It may possibly be significant that there is no such note in the *Vita Aeschyli*. To judge from the *Catalogue*, only one play in the Aeschylean corpus was recognized as spurious in antiquity: a "spurious *Aitnaiai*," detection of which must have been easy because a "genuine *Aitnaiai*" evidently still existed, and was catalogued alongside it.

[5] Individual scholars could of course make horrible mistakes, then as now; witness the superb story of the trick played on Heracli-

As a class, they had infinitely more material before them than we do; in evaluating it they paid attention both to linguistic details and to general stylistic considerations; if they had doubts as to a play's authenticity, they expressed them vociferously; those doubts, even with regard to plays now lost, tend to be preserved in our *Vitae,* scholia, and hypotheses; and not a trace of doubt is recorded with regard to a play as famous as the *Prometheus.*

From this consideration and from the positive evidence of the *Catalogue* and the scholia I conclude that no ancient scholar of any eminence hesitated in attributing the *Prometheus* to Aeschylus. One could hardly ask for more authoritative external testimony. If it is to be rejected, the grounds for rejection must be overwhelmingly strong.

2. Once one has abandoned the external testimony, for whatever reasons, then the question whether Poem *A* can be the work of Poet *X* surely becomes to a great extent subjective. It now implies no less than this: What in the poem is characteristic or uncharacteristic (*a*) of the poet's artistic personality, (*b*) of the poet himself, as far as his career and circumstances can be reconstructed? By "artistic

---

des Ponticus by a dastardly associate (Diogenes Laertius 5.92–93). The numerous errors in attribution committed by Callimachus are collected by Dover, pp. 23 ff. But one should note (*a*) that those errors mostly concerned the orators, who presented much more difficult problems from this point of view, and (*b*) that when Callimachus blundered over a *poet,* such as Pindar or Aristophanes, his mistakes were pounced on by other Alexandrian scholars in short order.

personality" I mean the sum of characteristics that can be sensed from the poet's extant *oeuvre*. That such a thing exists no one who reads literature can deny. Nor can he deny that an artistic personality may be as immediately identifiable as a living personality. A line in poetry, an action in life, though containing no definable element repeated from elsewhere, may be such that one will say, without a second thought, "That is characteristic of *X* or *Y*."

In method, the poet and his artistic personality should generally be kept distinct, above all when the poet in question is a dramatist. Judging from modern authors whose *oeuvre* and personal life are both well documented, I conclude that the relation between the two cannot be predicted a priori; they may overlap almost perfectly, or there may be almost no discernible connection between them. (One of my main complaints against Schmid is his failure either to observe this distinction consistently, or to remember that Aeschylus is a dramatist, or to observe that the statement of antithetical positions is not only inherent in all drama, but also essential to the grand structure of the only complete Aeschylean trilogy that we possess. Too often I seem to hear below his learned argument a sotto voce rhetorical question: "Could the whiskered and intrepid hero of Marathon have spoken with the voice of such a *Jammermann* as Prometheus?" This makes no more sense than "Could Ann Hathaway's husband have created Beatrice?")

If this formulation is correct, the difficulty of finding objective criteria must be frankly recognized; for objective, or tolerably objective, criteria are what must be found if the aim is a discussion rather than a shouting match. I cannot think that Schmid, or many others who have discussed problems of this sort, grasped the scale of the difficulty. The variables in an artistic personality may be no fewer than those to be observed in the living individual. And the mightier the poet concerned, the more experimental his art, the greater his mastery of his medium, the more turbulent the political and intellectual atmosphere of his lifetime, then the more variables may be expected.

Applying these principles specifically to Aeschylus, we may well shudder. All the factors just enumerated are present. As if that were not enough, the modern world possessed, until about a century ago, only one-tenth, or less,[6] of Aeschylus' plays complete. What has become available since, through the discovery of papyri and the systematic publication of the fragments, has been quantitatively rather little— but that little has been enough to push further and further outward the conceivable boundaries of Aeschylus' imagination and technique. I need do no more than recall the *Glaukos Pontios,* the Achilles tetralogy, the *Aitnaiai,* the *Kabeiroi,* the *Diktyoulkoi,* or the fire song from a *Prometheus* (*Pyrkaeus?*). On such fragmentary evidence as we have, can we even begin to construct the required artistic

---

[6] This depends on whether one accepts the total of 75 plays given (probably) in the *Vita Aeschyli,* or the total of 90 given in the *Suda.* The evidence, as far as it goes, suggests to me that the *Suda* is more likely to be right.

personality against which to compare the *Prometheus?* The data for the poet's external circumstances are more fragmentary still. Practically all we can tell about the last two decades of his life is that his city, and the Sicilian cities that he visited, were moving fast through a crisis, intellectual, social, and political, such as the Western world can perhaps never know again. The exact dates and details of the process, however, are almost all beyond recovery; the chief exceptions being in fact the productions of the plays of Aeschylus, and those plays themselves. In short, the conditions in this case are abnormally unfavorable for the reconstruction of either the author's life or of his artistic personality.

That is, I hope, a fair estimate of the scale of the problem before us. I will not disguise my uncertainty as to whether a generally acceptable solution can ever be found on the available evidence. For we are not here, I think, to construct artificial methods for the convenience of professional problem solvers; we are here to seek, in all seriousness and humility, the truth about a tragedy that has probably transcended more ideological and racial boundaries than any other work of classical imaginative literature. And it is not merely an author's name that is now at stake; it is the interpretation of an entire play.

In view of the material that time has left, it seems that the investigation will have to be confined to the comparison of the *Prometheus* with the extant artistic personality of Aeschylus. Only at the very end shall I call upon the scanty biographical and historical information.

At first view, the one constant factor in Aeschylus' artistic personality is its versatility! This is seen right across the spectrum of possible artistic expression: in meter, diction, ad hoc word creation, ad hoc creation of external dramatic forms to match dramatic ideas,[7] and the dramatic ideas themselves. Such *total* versatility cannot be matched in ancient tragedy. In my experience it is approached only by Aristophanes.

Strangely enough, it is at this black moment that I see the first gleam of hope for this enquiry. One can show that the full range of Aristophanes' versatility is not apparent at any one moment in his career.[8] *An artistic personality, that*

[7] I think, in particular, of the unique external form—simply unrepeatable in any other dramatic situation—of the Shield Scene in the *Septem*, and of the *Supplices* in its entirety. The pattern of the former ultimately depends on no a priori theory of dramaturgy, but on the brute fact that heroic Thebes had seven gates! The pattern of the latter, I believe, may depend ultimately on the mythic datum that Danaus begot not one refugee-suppliant-murderess, but a host of them. In both plays the apparent limitations imposed by the myth, far from being evaded, are actually seized on and transfigured into dramatic virtues.

[8] For a very brief sketch, cf. *Phoenix* 19 (1965) 322. To me, the artistic personality of Euripides develops in a somewhat similar way. R. K. Sherk's article in *Arethusa* I (1968) 103 ff. reminds me that we have explicit ancient testimony in Plutarch's *Aristoph. et Menand. Comp.* to Menander's development: εἰ οὖν πρὸς τὰ πρῶτα τῶν Μενάνδρου δραμάτων τὰ μέσα καὶ τὰ τελευταῖα παραβάλοι τις, ἐξ αὐτῶν ἐπιγνώσεται ὅσα ἔμελλεν ··· προσθήσειν.

is, can change swiftly, and often radically, with time. Where
that process can be demonstrated, we are no longer con-
fronted with one massive, baffling congeries of characteristics
against which to compare the disputed work, but with a
succession of limited and manageable groups.

If I may take up again an analogy I have used elsewhere,[9]
I would ask the reader to imagine for a moment that we are
trying to check the authenticity of a picture alleged by the
dealer to have been painted by Picasso in 1937. If we checked
it against his earliest work, or even against his work of
fifteen or ten years before 1937, we should indignantly
demand our money back. The dealer might faintly point to
some resemblances in the brushwork, or vaguely speak of a
Weltanschauung common to our picture and the pictures
compared, but I fear he would obtain little mercy from a
court of law on those grounds. His only hope would be to
show that Picasso in fact evolved through seven or eight
strikingly different artistic personalities, sometimes with
baffling abruptness, and to lead us before the canvases of
the Spanish Civil War era, where we should see that not only
the techniques but also the themes match those of the suspected painting.

Examples could be multiplied indefinitely, as in this recent
biography of Aubrey Beardsley: "As with the *Salome,* which
encompassed a much briefer creative period, by the time
Beardsley had completed the project [illustrations to the
Morte d'Arthur] he had so outdistanced the phase of his

[9] Herington (IV) p. 388.

development in which he had begun it that he had to create forgeries of his earlier style in order to complete the work."[10]

Now the main contention of the present study is that, since the redating of the *Supplices*,[11] it becomes very likely if not certain that Aeschylus belongs to this species of artist; that, during the period when we can trace it, his artistic personality underwent an abrupt change. Here is a summary of the chronology of Aeschylus' work as it now appears to stand:

472: Phineus, *Persae*, Glaukos Potnieus, Prometheus (Pyrkaeus?)

467: Laius, Oedipus, *Septem*, Sphinx

466 or later (possibly 463): *Supplices*, Aigyptioi, Danaides, Amymone

458: *Agamemnon, Choephori, Eumenides,* Proteus

---

[10] S. Weintraub, *Beardsley* (New York, 1967) 81.

[11] The best discussion of this question that I know is by H. Lloyd-Jones, Appendix to H. W. Smyth's *Aeschylus*, vol. II (2nd ed., 1957) pp. 595–596. I have only one point to add to it. The dating of the play precisely to the year 463 (a dating that seems to become increasingly common in the handbooks) depends on the assumption that $\epsilon\pi\iota\alpha$ in the first line of the papyrus must be the remains of the formula ἐπὶ 'Αρχεδημίδου (archon 464/3). Perhaps it is necessary to stress once more that this assumption is not certain, though the statistical odds in favor of it are about 2 to 1. In the majority of our extant hypotheses the date formula is either ἐπὶ XYZ ἄρχοντος or simply ἐπὶ XYZ. But in a substantial minority (Hypoth. *Agam.*, Hypoth II *OC*, Hypoth V *Nub.* init., I *Vesp.*, I *Pax*) the formula is ἐπὶ ἄρχοντος XYZ. Until it can be *proved* that the papyrus cannot imply the latter formula, I think that the exact date 463 should certainly be accompanied by a question mark.

I would also recall at this point that Aeschylus left Athens shortly after the production of the *Oresteia* and took up residence in Sicily, where he died in 456/5.[12] Now by a simple and unavoidably crude calculation Aeschylus composed, on the average, one tetralogy for every two years of his career; and indeed one might doubt on general grounds whether the frequency of production could ever have much exceeded that.[13] This means that since the redating of the *Supplices* we have specimens, at least, of a relatively high proportion of the trilogies probably produced by Aeschylus during the fourteen years 472–458 B.C. If his artistic personality did in fact change during this period, we should now have enough evidence to follow that process, at least in outline.

I think we can. With some confidence, we can break down the extant *oeuvre* into two phases: first, *c.* 472 to 467 (*Pe, Se*); second, *c.* 466 or later to 458 (*Su, Oresteia*). Elsewhere I have already published some tentative arguments for this grouping,[14] which I hope may be reinforced by the following chapters. At this point I would only emphasize that, if the theory is anywhere near the truth, the conditions of the authenticity problem are revolutionized. We need no longer ask (as, whether they fully realized it or not, previous in-

[12] See Herington (VI), p. 76, for review of the evidence.

[13] In passing, we may recall that a single comedy cost Cratinus, by his own account, two years' labor (*Cheirones,* Fr. 237 K).

[14] Primarily in Herington (IV); cf. also (V) pp. 113–115 and (VI) pp. 80–81.

vestigators had to ask) what elements in the *Prometheus* are characteristic or uncharacteristic of a vast, static, indefinable artistic personality, the elements for the reconstruction of which are nine-tenths lost. The question is now rephrased to become: *Does the Prometheus accord with either of the two distinct phases of Aeschylus' artistic personality, for both of which we have (relatively) abundant evidence?* If it accords with neither phase, we shall of course be much as we were, with perhaps an increased presumption in favor of spuriousness. But if it accords very closely with the works of one or the other of the two phases, then the questions both of date and of authenticity will be very much nearer a satisfying solution.

It is in this context that I now define the main criteria that I shall adopt in analyzing the *Prometheus* and in making the comparisons:

a) Minor features of diction, style, meter, and composition (Chapter II)

b) The view of the cosmos implied in the several plays and reflected in their composition (Chapter III)

That is, I am taking two tests at opposite extremes: stylistic "tics" and mannerisms at the unconscious or barely conscious level of composition, and features that certainly belong to the conscious level, resulting as they must from deliberate artistic decisions on the grand scale. If the results of these two tests tend to coincide, then the presumption that our general theory is correct will be strengthened.

A test at any level between those two is, in my experience, very much more difficult to apply convincingly, because of Aeschylus' almost unlimited ability to conform his technique to his ideas. For instance, vocabulary counts and lists of words peculiar to the *Prometheus* (*Eigenwörter*), to which Niedzballa and Schmid—the latter more cautiously—paid so much attention, seem to me of little practical value as evidence.[15] It can always be objected with much show of reason that the choice (and often, in our poet, the ad hoc creation) of the words is directly conditioned by the matter of the drama; for example, the occurrence of αὐθάδης and derivatives eight times in the *PV* and nowhere else in Aeschylus is merely a function of the *PV*'s theme.[16]

The general argument from the simplicity and "limpidity" of the *PV*'s style breaks down against a similar objection. Perhaps the full diapason of Aeschylean style has never yet been listened to with enough attention. Compare the style of *Pe* (which approaches that of the *PV* in its epic simplicity and relatively low proportion of figurative speech) with the loaded, introvert style of *Se* or, still more, of *Ag*; or, within *Ag* alone, the range (according to mood and subject) from

[15] Young's excellent article (see Bibliography), in which he conclusively proved by similar means that *Paradise Regained* cannot be by the author of *Paradise Lost,* should stand forever as a dire warning to classical—and other—scholars.

[16] For the same reason, no doubt, αὐθάδης and derivatives occur four times in the *Medea,* but only thrice elsewhere in the entire Euripidean corpus (Page on *Med.* 1028).

popular love song,[17] through epic exposition, to the glories
of Pindaric choral lyric—or more than Pindaric. And yet
again, arguments from the general dramatic technique of the
PV (the unusual shortness of the choral odes, the alleged
episodic and static character of the action as a whole) can be
opposed on the same lines: What is the limit to Aeschylus'
technical range, even judging by the few plays we have?

I do not say that such arguments are without instruction or
interest, and I hope that I have not ignored any of their
major exponents in preparing to write this monograph. But
on the whole I do not find them probative enough for our
purposes, and I shall therefore concentrate mainly, though
not exclusively, on the two criteria defined above.

[17] e.g., 742–743: μαλθακὸν ὀμμάτων βέλος,
              δηξίθυμον ἔρωτος ἄνθος.
     "Gentle javelin of her eyes,
      stingheart flower of love."

CHAPTER II

First Criterion: Minor Stylistic and Metrical Phenomena

This chapter is essentially a checklist, with brief discussion and bibliographical notes, of certain striking stylistic and metrical phenomena in the *Prometheus* that I have collected from the publications, or—in a few instances—observed for myself. The list is subdivided in a sort of descending order, from those features that seem to be unique in all drama to those that the *PV* displays in common with *Su* and the *Oresteia*. The reader may find it helpful to refer to the table of contents at the beginning of the book and to the comparative tables in Chapter Five. I am sure that I will have included items here that will seem nonsignificant, and

omitted (or just failed to notice!) material some will think
of the highest importance. On such points I shall particularly
welcome correction.

1. *Unparalleled in Dramatic Poetry*

a) *Choric quatrains.* In *PV* the spoken (iambic) utterances
of the Chorus are confined to quatrains, apart from single
lines in stichomythia and the couplet 698–699. I know of no
parallels in drama at all, though a very slight inclination to
"choric quatrains" is visible in *Su* and *Oresteia* and is continued in later Attic tragedy (with the exception of Euripides'
last six plays).[1]

b) *Formal pattern in line arrangement.* I do not know of
any close parallel to the meticulous formalism seen in the
following passages of the *PV*, unless we admit the rather
remote parallel of the epirrhematic systems in Old Comedy.

511–525: quatrain (Prom.)—*seven* lines of stichomythia
    (Chor., Prom.)—quatrain (Prom.).

613–630: couplet (Io)—*seven* lines of stichomythia
    (Prom., Io)—couplet (Io)—*seven* lines of sticho-
    mythia. (*Seven* lines of stichomythia are found also
    in *PV* 386–392: Prom., Ocean. There are no seven-

---

[1] See Herington (II) for discussion and comparative figures.
Only long after I had written that note did I have the opportunity
to see Ribbeck's short tract, and so to learn that Ribbeck, and
Welcker before him, had discussed this phenomenon; neither of
them, however, applied it to the problems of date and authenticity.
Ribbeck has much of interest to say both on the quatrains and on
the formal patterns (see 1 *b*).

line blocks of stichomythia in the other plays of Aeschylus. The nearest parallel in Aeschylus to such a repetition of stichomythiae of identical length occurs in *Ag*,
where three consecutive stichomythiae consist of 13
lines: 268–280, 538–550, 931–943.)

1040–end (anapaests): Prom. 14 lines—Hermes 9—
Chorus 8—Hermes 9—Prom. 14. Regarded by Wecklein (I, ad loc.) and Smyth (p. 155) as an instance of
strophic responsion in anapaests: *a b–mesode– b a*. I do
not find this particularly convincing, but at all events,
as Smyth notes, this would be "the only certain case . . .
in closing anapaests."

Compare also (*a*), immediately above; and perhaps the
1:2 stichomythia (below 3 *e*).

c) *Unparalleled frequency of word and phrase repetition*.
Insistent repetition within a single poem or passage is of
course a common literary phenomenon that can be illustrated
from all the plays of Aeschylus. I would instance πολύχρυσος
(four times in *Pe* 1–53, nowhere else in the Aeschylean
corpus). But Schmid was no doubt justified in treating the
high frequency of repetition in *PV* as a unique feature.
Though exact comparative statistics seem to be lacking,
there is almost certainly nothing approaching a parallel in
tragedy or comedy.

Schmid's lists should be consulted (I, pp. 9–11, 46, 68–71,
74–76). But they should also be carefully checked; Schmid
did not have the benefit of Italie! Thus, when he notes (his
p. 71) that *PV* uses πρὸς βίαν four times, and that this phrase

is never found in "Aeschylus" ("Aeschylean" for "by force" being βίᾳ or βιαίως), one is duly impressed—until Italie reveals that πρὸς βίαν occurs twice in the *Oresteia*. Furthermore, each instance of repetition should be most carefully and delicately weighed with reference to the play as a whole. The possibility that at least some of the repetitions might constitute a deliberate stylistic device uniquely adapted to *PV*'s theme (are not pain and time per se repetitious?) had indeed occurred to Schmid, but I cannot believe that he gave it enough thought.

Here, for example, is an addition to Schmid's list that I am sure he would have welcomed. The participle παρών occurs ten times in *PV with the definite article in the attributive position* (as 392 τὸν παρόντα νοῦν).[2] There is only a single parallel in all the rest of Aeschylus: *Pe* 825 τὸν παρόντα δαίμονα. Is this another instance of the stylistic poverty of an atheistical Ionian technologist (or whoever it was who wrote *PV* according to Schmid)? Or is it rather a subliminal reassurance to the spectator of the trilogy that Prometheus' agony will not endure forever? In the latter case, of course, it also constitutes a scrap of additional evidence for the reconstruction of the trilogy.

One final remark on the repetitions: If the *Bound* is to be athetized on this ground, we ought logically to athetize the

[2] The instances are: *PV* 26, 47, 98, 271, 313–314, 375, 392, 471, 971, 1000. Perhaps 321 should be added as an eleventh. All refer to the sufferings of Prometheus, except for 392. In 47, 313–314, 471 the idea is strengthened by the addition of νῦν.

Unbound as well—in spite of Schmid's passionate belief in the latter's authenticity (I, pp. 97f., 106ff.). For there is good reason for thinking that the frequency of repetition was no lower in that play than in the extant *Prometheus*.[3]

2. *Unparalleled in Tragedy*

a) Initial rho *preceded by a short vowel not constituting a long syllable.* Maas (para. 130; comparing Meineke III, pp. 303–304, which is still the fullest discussion of the question) cites two passages in *PV* as the only two certain instances of this phenomenon in tragic or comic iambic verse. If Maas is correct, then this item should belong to section 1, above. But the situation is obscure. The instances in *PV* are:

713 (Io scene) χρίμπτουσα ῥαχίαισιν.

992 (Exodus) πρὸς ταῦτα ῥιπτέσθω.

The other instances offered by the MSS in tragedy and comedy, as far as I know, are:

Lyric: *Se* 93 ἄρα ῥύσεται; Eur. *Supplices* 380 πάντα ῥύῃ, *Bacchae* 128 τε Ῥέας; Ar. *Wasps* 1067 τῶνδε ῥώμην.[4]

Iambic: *Eu* 232 τε ῥύσομαι; Soph. *OT* 72 τήνδε ῥυσαίμην (so most MSS; a few read τήνδ' ἐρυσαίμην); Eur. *Bacchae* 59 τύμπανα Ῥέας, *Bacchae* 1338 τε ῥύσεται.

[3] Details in Herington (I), pp. 240–241, 249–250. Cf. below, Chapter V 6, for other rare stylistic details common to the *Bound* and the *Unbound*.

[4] White (p. 366) considered this to be the only certain instance in Aristophanes. For four other possible instances in comedy generally, all disputed, see Meineke.

Anapaests: *Se* 824 τούσδε ῥύεσθε (doubtful, because the context is corrupt).[5]

It will be noticed that all the instances involve the always recalcitrant verb ῥύομαι, except for two of the *Bacchae* passages, which have the proper name 'Ρέας,[6] and the *Wasps* passage. In fact the last, alone, shares with the two *PV* passages the peculiarity of possessing one of these metrically peccant *rho*'s in a perfectly ordinary word.

The evidence is both scanty and disputed, but from what there is I would judge that the only passage in all drama that offers a really close parallel to these in *PV* is *Wasps* 1067, though even that is lyric, not iambic. Very tentatively, therefore, I would suggest that *PV* 713 and 992 may be instances of an affinity with (or influence by?) comic style; such an affinity will appear very clearly in the next item. The even less likely alternative might be to add the two passages to the list of Ionisms or epicisms in the *PV* compiled by Römer (pp. 206–207), for of course initial *rho* need not "make position" in epic verse. If so, they would be the only *metrical*

---

[5] Most of these instances were collected by Hermann on Soph. *OT* 72.

[6] Maas emended all the passages with ῥύομαι by substituting ἐρύομαι and followed Nauck in emending *Bacchae* 59 to τύπανα 'Ρέας. I always admire a tidy mind, myself! But this wholesale condemnation of the MSS—or rather, except in the last case, of the word division in the MSS—is a little too much for me; and I was glad to find that Dodds (on *Bacchae* 1338) is also reluctant to accept it.

epicisms in the play. Whatever the explanation, however, the clear fact remains that the passages are unique in tragedy.

b) Interlinear hiatus after trimeters without stop. Of all the minor stylistic mannerisms that have been observed in *PV*, the one that I now discuss is the most extraordinary; but it seems to have received no attention in this context since it was first pointed out by Harrison in 1941. The reader should, if possible, consult Harrison's article for himself. In the following summary I necessarily omit most of the very careful justification and qualification with which the author guarded his remarks. But I do not think that there can be any doubt at all—even when one has conceded the difficulty of objectively deciding whether many lines should rank as stopped or not—about the general validity of his observation and conclusions.

According to Harrison, then, hiatus between the end of one trimeter and the beginning of the next (e.g., τοιᾶσδέ τοι / ἁμαρτίας, *PV* 8-9) is per se apparently a haphazard phenomenon in tragedy, depending on no more than the mathematical probability that a certain proportion of lines beginning with a vowel will follow lines ending with a vowel. Thus in the 773 trimeters of *PV* there are 130 interlinear hiatuses; and in the 969 trimeters of Soph. *Trach.* there are 150. The picture, however, becomes entirely different when one studies the incidence of interlinear hiatus where the first of the two lines concerned in each case *has no stop at the end*, a phenomenon that I will hereafter call, for

short, "nonstop hiatus."[7] Harrison's figures, which he published in some detail for Sophocles and Euripides but not
(unfortunately) for Aeschylus, indicated that, throughout
all extant tragedy, there is a definite and no doubt conscious
tendency to restrict this phenomenon. In Sophocles' *Antigone*
and *Trachiniae,* for example, each with over 900 trimeters,
he found only eight and six instances, respectively, of nonstop hiatus. In Euripides, his figures for each tragedy are in
the teens or twenties, until the plays of the poet's last decade,
when they rise considerably;[8] the highest number in any
Euripidean play is found in the *Helena* (1267 trimeters, 58
nonstop hiatuses).

But Harrison found one startling exception: *In the "PV"
the tendency just described did not seem to be operating at
all.* He concludes: "It seems that in this play such [interlinear] hiatus occurs indifferently whether the line ends with
a stop or no." The only parallels that he offers—again, unfortunately, without publishing his figures—are Aristophanes' *Acharnians* and, more definitely, *Knights.*

---

[7] This terminology is of course convenient rather than strictly
accurate. Since the original texts of the tragedies (like the copies of
them for centuries afterward) presumably had little or no punctuation, we should really speak not of "stops" but of "grammatical
pauses," such as the ends of clauses or periods. Of course modern
editors will vary to some extent when it comes to indicating such
breaks by means of postclassical punctuation marks, but the uncertainty factor thereby created is not very great.

[8] Thus to some extent paralleling the increase in resolved feet
observed in Euripides' verse at this period (Ceadel, esp. p. 70).

TABLE 1

I. Number of trimeters	II. Instances of interlinear hiatus (all kinds)	III. Instances of nonstop hiatus
AESCHYLUS		
Pe 429	78 (18% of I)	19 (24.5% of II)
Se 515	84 (16.5%)	15 (18%)
Su 400	62 (15.5%)	12 (19.5%)
Ag 843	142 (17%)	31 (23%)
Ch 621	104 (16.5%)	17 (16.5%)
Eu 641	120 (18.5%)	24 (20%)
PV 773	129 (16.5%)	53 (41%)
ARISTOPHANES		
Acharnians 817	133 (16% of I)	26 (19.5% of II)
Knights 688	111 (16%)	47 (42.5%)
Wasps 758	144 (19%)	46 (32%)
Clouds 757	134 (17.5%)	42 (31.5%)
Peace 700	117 (16.5%)	42 (36%)

Recently S. B. B. Carleton, of The University of Texas at Austin, and I made some attempt to control and amplify Harrison's statistics. In Table 1 the figures for Aeschylus are Mr. Carleton's and are based primarily on the second-edition Oxford text (1955); the figures for Aristophanes were compiled by me on the basis of Coulon's Budé text. In Column II the percentages in parentheses show the proportion of interlinear hiatuses (all kinds) to the number of trimeters in each play, as given in Column I. In Column III the percentages in parentheses show the proportion of nonstop hiatuses to the total number of hiatuses (all kinds) as given in Column II. All percentages are given to the nearest half of 1 percent.

On the whole, these figures bear out Harrison's thesis. It will be noticed that the percentages for interlinear hiatus of all kinds (Col. II) remain practically constant in both the playwrights, 3.5 percent being the widest variation. But the percentages for nonstop hiatus (Col. III) show a very wide variation—wide enough to be significant beyond any doubt whatever, even when one allows, as one should, for the likelihood that no two qualified observers would produce exactly the same totals of this slightly elusive phenomenon. Here six of Aeschylus' plays conform to the tendency observed by Harrison in tragedy generally, in that they severely restrict the number of nonstop hiatuses. *PV*, however, drops completely out of the Aeschylean—and tragic!—pattern. It has, in fact, the highest proportion of all the plays studied, except the *Knights*. (Why the *Acharnians*, for its part, should range itself alongside the *Supplices* I do not know. Its high content of tragic parody, or of dialect, might possibly be responsible; but only further and very delicate study, passage by passage, could decide the point.)

3. Unparalleled in the Extant Plays and Fragments of Aeschylus

a) *Uses of the definite article.* I include this item tentatively, since a full investigation (which is highly desirable) would require a tract in itself. As far as I know, however, the following are unique in Aeschylus:

(1) Article in idiomatic expressions stressing the length of time or life: *PV* 94–95 τὸν μυριετῆ χρόνον, 449 τὸν μακρὸν βίον, 538 τὸν μακρὸν τείνειν βίον.

Parallels: Pindar, *Ol.* 2.30 τὸν ὅλον ἀμφὶ χρόνον (I owe this reference to Prof. S. Benardete); Soph. *Aj.* 342/3 τὸν εἰσαεὶ . . . χρόνον, 473 τοῦ μακροῦ χρήζειν βίου, 646 ὁ μακρὸς κἀναρίθμητος χρόνος, *OT* 518; Ar. *Wasps* 1006 τὸν λοιπὸν χρόνον; Thuc. 4.117 τὸν πλείω χρόνον.

(2) *PV* 1038 τὴν σοφὴν εὐβουλίαν. Presumably this phrase is an instance of the article not used attributively, but to point out a well-known characteristic of the noun (Smyth, *Gk. Grammar,* para. 1160). But with this particular noun and this particular adjective the effect is very strange. The only parallels I have found are Xenophanes B2 lines 3–4 τῆς ἀγαθῆς σοφίης, and Eur. *Heraclidae* 109–110:

καλὸν δέ γ' ἔξω πραγμάτων ἔχειν πόδα,[9]
εὐβουλίας τυχόντα τῆς ἀμείνονος.

There is a family resemblance between the three passages in thought as well as in words, but I do not yet see how to interpret it.

b) High proportion of resultative perfects. This factor in the problem has been with us since (to be precise) Friday, October 4, 1901, when Wackernagel (I) unveiled it in an

---

[9] A reminiscence of *PV* 263?

oration at Strasbourg. Since then it has been discussed by, among others, Focke (pp. 298–299), Chantraine (pp. 119 ff.), Peretti (pp. 205–207), Schmid (I, p. 2, n. 4), and Coman (pp. 100 ff.).

Wackernagel maintained that primitive Greek used the perfect formation only to express a *state* confined to the subject; it did not know that temporal and transitive meaning, whereby "das Perfekt von einer vergangenen Handlung gebraucht wird, deren Wirkung im oder am Objekt noch in der Gegenwart fortdauert."[10] For example, as he pointed out, no perfect is found in epic Greek for verbs of inherently resultative meaning, such as τίθημι and δίδωμι; even in classical Greek the expression for "parents" remained the ancient aorist οἱ τεκόντες, instead of οἱ τετοκότες (which the analogy of later Greek generally would have led us to expect). Although Wackernagel's thesis has been modified by later discussions, and although in practice it is not always easy to decide whether a given perfect is resultative or not, his general observation seems to remain valid; and so does his observation that this usage made its way rather slowly into the mainland Greek of the early fifth century. Here are the statistics for its occurrence in fifth-century poetry, as they now seem to stand:[11]

[10] Wackernagel (II) p. 4. Chantraine (p. 122) offers this alternative description of the new usage: "Le parfait exprime bien encore un état; mais ce n'est plus l'état du sujet, c'est celui de l'objet."

[11] The references, of course, include resultative pluperfects as well as perfects. With the exceptions shortly to be noted, I rely on the

Pindar: two undisputed instances (*Nem.* 2.8, *Isthm.* 4.37); two or three less certain instances might be added.

Aeschylus: *Pe*, none; *Se*, two (583, 821); *Su*, one (246); *Ag*, one (267); *Ch*, none; *Eu*, two (57, 587); *PV*, at least five (211, 446, 586, 740, 821); Fragments, at least one (618.2 M).[12]

Sophocles: Chantraine lists twenty-five instances, distributed thus: *Aj.* one; *Ant.* four; *Trach.* five; *OT* five; *El.* two; *Phil.* three; *OC* three; Fragments two.

Euripides: Chantraine actually lists only twenty instances; but perhaps did not intend the figure to be exhaustive, since on page 128 he says that this type of perfect is "usuel" in Euripides.

Aristophanes: Chantraine found no less than 208 instances here (p. 136).

I have tried to control Chantraine's statistics only in Aeschylus, not in the other four authors concerned. Three of his Aeschylean instances seemed so doubtful that I have excluded them from the above list. They are (1) *Se* 423 Καπανεὺς δ' ἐπ' Ἠλέκτραισιν εἴληχεν πύλαις, where the object (even if an object need be supplied at all)[13] could scarcely

---

list given by Chantraine, pp. 123–127; Coman (pp. 100 ff.) adds some putative instances, none of them convincing.

[12] There is another certain instance in Fr. 609.2 M, but Oder (cited by Wackernagel II, p. 11) showed strong linguistic reasons for denying this fragment to Aeschylus.

[13] Italie was no doubt right to include this passage among his seven Aeschylean instances of λαγχάνω used *absolutely*.

be said to be affected by the verb; I would render simply "his lot is at the Electran Gate." (2) *PV* 51 ἔγνωκα τοῖσδε where, again, a grammatical object need not even be supplied, and the verb surely expresses the state of the *subject*. (3) *PV* 825 ἃ πρὶν μολεῖν δεῦρ' ἐκμεμόχθηκεν φράσω, where the accusative is not objective, but cognate (equivalent to μόχθους οὓς), and therefore adverbial in function. It also seems debatable whether verbs of speaking or perception can ever have a "resultative" force by Wackernagel's definition; but I have allowed Chantraine's four instances (*Su* 246 εἴρηκας, *Eu* 57 ὄπωπα, *PV* 740 ἀκήκοας, *PV* 821 εἴρηκας) to stand in the list, on the ground that they certainly represent a new development of the perfect, and one that is closely allied to the resultative use.

By any analysis, however, *PV* contains more resultative perfects than any other Aeschylean play, and at least as many as the average extant tragedy of Sophocles. The natural conclusion from this, and from the rest of Wackernagel's evidence, is that *PV* is later than Aeschylus' latest dated work, the *Oresteia*.

c) High proportion of first-foot anapaests in the trimeters (proper names excluded). I give the figures after Yorke (I), p. 118. Ceadel (p. 84) offers slightly different figures, for methodic reasons that he explains (p. 84, n. 1). On the whole I prefer Yorke's method in this matter.

Two instances of first-foot anapaests in each of the following: *Pe, Se, Su, Ch*; six instances in *Ag*; three instances in

Eu; twelve instances in *PV;* six certain instances in the fragments—one of them from the *Unbound*.[14]

This striking disproportion was first noticed by G. Hermann, and has been much discussed since—not always by
well-qualified persons.[15] It is so great that I am not sure
whether this item ought not to be placed in section 2 of this
chapter, rather than here. On Ceadel's calculation (based,
for *PV,* on the same absolute figure as Yorke's), 32 percent
of *all* resolved feet in the *PV* are first-foot anapaests. The
highest corresponding percentage in Sophocles is found in
OT and *Phil.* (both 14 percent); in Euripides it is 18 percent
(*Alcestis*; the runners-up are *Cyclops* and *Heraclidae,* each
with 16 percent).

Focke (p. 249) suggested, without giving statistics, that

---

[14] The figures for the fragments are my own. As certain instances
I count: *Unbound* 326.7 M, *Philoctetes* 397 and 401, *Mysians* 413.1,
Dike-drama 530.9, Inc. Fab. 601.1. In the following fragments some
editors have restored a corrupt or incomplete text in such a way
that a first-foot anapaest results: satyr-play *Theoroi* 17.36, *Cares or
Europa* 145.22, Dike-drama 530.1. Following Yorke and Ceadel, I
do not take proper names into account, but to complete the statistics I add that they occur in first-foot anapaests at Fr. 145.12 M,
275.2, 278c.2, 329.3.

[15] I note Coman's discussion (pp. 143–144) during which he
scans the opening of *PV* 12 as Κρᾰτⁱος / Βῐᾰ τ / and triumphantly
cites this monster as an instance of an anapaest in the second foot.
In general, Coman's book is a useful compilation of evidence bearing on the problem, but I have found that each fact and argument
in it needs double checking.

the nearest parallels were to be found in satyr-play and comedy. Ceadel's statistics for the *Cyclops* now make satyr-play a little less likely (his absolute figure for first-foot anapaests in that play is thirty-three, but resolution at all points is far above average there). The nearest parallel that I have found is in the fragments of Epicharmus (see end of Chapter Six).

d) *High proportion of enjambment.*

Type: *PV* 61–62 καὶ τήνδε νῦν πόρπασον ἀσφαλῶς, ἵνα

μάθῃ σοφιστὴς ὢν Διὸς νωθέστερος.

I begin by reproducing the figures from Yorke (II). Yorke defines the phenomenon thus: "Consecutive trimeters closely [knitted] together by placing at the end of one line some word which looks forward to the next line, and so precludes the reader from stopping for the natural pause after the sixth foot" (p. 153). His figures are:

Pe: one (line 486, Μηλιᾶτε κόλπον, οὗ/); *Se, Su*: none; *Oresteia*: seven; *PV*: eighteen certain examples at least, "distributed evenly over the dialogue passages"; or, on average, once in every forty-three trimeters. Such enjambment is common in Sophocles, being found on average once in every forty-five or fifty of his trimeters; the average in *Ajax* and *Electra* is in fact lower than in *PV*. It is, on the other hand, rare in Euripides, who can show only "about 30 examples altogether." On these grounds Yorke argued that the *PV* must have been composed later than the *Oresteia*, adding, "I do not consider the possibility of dating the *Prometheus* before the *Septem* since, among other reasons, this would involve a quite incredible series of changes in Aeschylus' metrical style" (p. 154, n. 2).

After checking for myself the incidence of enjambment in all three Attic tragedians (using the Oxford texts in each case), I agree with Yorke's general statement of the facts. There is need, however, for a few modifications in detail:

(1) Yorke accepts as examples not only *single words* standing at the end of a trimeter (e.g., ἐπεί, ἵνα, ὅτι), but also a few *groups* of closely associated monosyllables (τί δ' οὐ, τὸ μὴ οὐ, τὸ μή). This seems legitimate, since the forward-leading effect is identical in both types. In that case, Yorke's definition, given at the head of this section, should be modified; and we should also add the passages discussed here in (2) and (3).

(2) σὺ δέ, preceded by a grammatical pause and leading into a fresh line containing an imperative, occurs four times in Aeschylus: *Su* 772; *PV* 43, 961, 1033.[16]

(3) τί γάρ, preceded by a grammatical pause and leading into a question in the following line(s). There are two instances in the *Oresteia*: *Ag* 601, *Ch* 702. (I exclude, of

---

[16] It will be noticed that the instances in the *PV* are found only in the Prologue and Exodus, thus conforming to a familiar pattern. The distribution of enjambment with σὺ δέ in the rest of Attic drama (excluding the last six plays of Aristophanes, from *Birds* onward, which I have not checked) is curious. Sophocles: two instances in *Ajax*, four in *Electra*, none in the other five plays (except possibly the corrupt passage *OC* 1209–1210). No instance in Euripides. Aristophanes: one in *Wasps*, two in *Clouds*.

course, τί γάρ used absolutely, without a following question, as at *Ch* 880).

(4) Five of Yorke's instances of enjambment in *PV* involve the conjunction ὅτι (104, 259, 328, 377, 951). It may be worth noticing that in all those passages, except 259, ὅτι introduces a resounding *gnomē* or general statement. This highly effective rhetorical device is not found elsewhere in Aeschylus (the ὅτι in enjambment at *Eu* 98 introduces a plain fact, not a *gnomē*), but is often used by Sophocles: *Electra* 988; *Ant.* 188, 311, 325, 649, 779, 1043; *Trach.* 439. Euripides also uses it, but only in his earlier phase: *Medea* 560 (cf., for related forms of expression, *Cyclops* 421 and *Alcestis* 418). This form of enjambment in *PV* is therefore closely linked to another peculiar feature of the play, which has long been noticed: its unusually large number of *gnomai*.[17]

To sum up, I find myself in agreement with Yorke's statistics and conclusions, except that I would add one instance of enjambment in the *Su*, two in the *Oresteia*, and three in *PV*. The story these figures tell is one that will become increasingly familiar as this investigation goes on: *PV* re-

---

[17] Schmid counted no less than 21 *gnomai* in *PV* (see Schmid I, p. 63 and n. 1), expressing a certain disapproval thereat. It might be worth considering whether the high incidence of *gnomai* introduced by ὅτι in the *PV* and *Antigone* is not due to the fact that both dramas are studies in tyranny. For tyranny, as the totalitarian régimes have shown in our time and as the *Antigone* has shown for all time, seems to flourish above all in an atmosphere of flat generalization.

peatedly seems to carry further a tendency already seen in *Su* and *Oresteia*. In this case, however, where the tendency is carried so far that it actually lands *PV*, statistically, among the plays of Sophocles, a caution may be in place. *PV*'s employment of this relatively unsubtle type of enjambment would by no means warrant the sweeping conclusion that the general texture of its verse resembles at all the texture of Sophoclean verse. It is a pleasant and instructive pastime to compare from this point of view any twenty consecutive lines of *PV* with any twenty consecutive Sophoclean lines. The Sophoclean verses will be found to cling together, in grammar and rhythm, like drowning swimmers, whereas *PV*'s verse shows the same distinct and majestic articulation that is characteristic of the other six plays of Aeschylus.

e) *1:2 stichomythia* (Hephaistos and Kratos, *PV* 39–81). This extraordinarily effective stylization, whereby the physically or emotionally engaged character speaks one line against the other character's two, is not paralleled in Aeschylean iambics. Elsewhere in ancient tragedy there are close parallels at Soph. *Aj.* 791–802 (Messenger 2: Tecmessa 1), and Seneca, *Oedipus* 509–522 (Oedipus 2: Creon 1). A possible parallel in Old Comedy is at Ar. *Peace* 439–452, though in that passage there seems to be no contrast between the speakers' respective physical or emotional states.[18]

This phenomenon is perhaps foreshadowed in the Aeschy-

[18] The speakers are not identifiable with certainty, though most editors assume that they are Hermes and Trygaeus (Platnauer on *Peace* 441–452).

lean passages *Su* 903–910 (Herald 2 trimeters: Chorus 1 dochmiac line) and *Eu* 117–130 (Ghost of Clytaemnestra 2 trimeters: Chorus, various animal grunts and 1 lyric line). But it will be noted that neither passage is purely iambic, so that the highly formal effect of the passages cited in the last paragraph is lacking.

Finally I should refer the reader to Jens' book on stichomythia (pp. 29–33 on *PV*). Primarily on the grounds—which, to me, are not sufficiently convincing—that the content and function of the stichomythiae are in some respects unlike those of the stichomythiae in Aeschylus' six other extant plays, he is inclined to athetize the *Prometheus*. He has not much to say on what seem to me the far more striking differences in formal line arrangement.[19]

f) Metron overlap in anapaestic dimeters. PV 172: καί μ' οὔτι μελι- / γλώσσοις πειθοῦς. Fraenkel (on *Ag* 52) pointed out that this was the only instance of *two*-syllable overlap in the extant plays of Aeschylus. From the fragments, however, he cites *Prometheus Unbound* Fr. 192 N (=323 M) line 4, λίμναν παντο- / τρόφον Αἰθιόπων. Unless that line is corrupt—which I doubt—this is another instance of a very rare stylistic peculiarity common to the *Bound* and *Unbound* (cf. below,

---

[19] His claim (p. 29) that the only Aeschylean parallel to a stichomythia near the opening of a play is the satyric *Diktyoulkoi* should be modified. (*a*) It is not quite certain (though I agree that it is likely) that *Diktyoulkoi* Fr. 464 M is from the end of the prologue; and (*b*) we should probably add the tragedy *Phryges* (Fr. 243 *a* M) to the list.

Chapter V, 6). It seems in fact to be unparalleled outside these two plays; even Sophocles, *Trach.* 985, cited here by Fraenkel, is different in that it is a *lyric* anapaest, and therefore is subject to different laws.[20]

g) *Dactylo-epitrite meter* (in the two odes framing the Io scene, *PV* 526 ff., 887 ff.). This striking meter (which seems almost to have formed a separate branch of music, with its own peculiar laws of composition) occurs nowhere else in the Aeschylean corpus.[21]

The next occurrence in tragedy, on the prevailing relative dating of Sophocles' plays, is at *Ajax* 172 ff.; after that it is often found in both Sophocles and Euripides. With Pindar, of course, it is a favorite rhythm; one might be tempted to connect its occurrence here with the two possible imitations of Pindaric descriptions at *PV* 351 ff., 922 ff.

4. *Confined to (or predominant in)* PV, Su, Oresteia

a) *Lieblingswörter.* Schmid (I, 74 ff.) collected an impressive list of these "favorite words" in *PV*, part of his case being that the mere excess of repetition told against the play's authenticity. On that point something has already been said

---

[20] See, e.g., W. S. Barrett, *Hippolytus* (Oxford, 1964), on *Hippol.* lines 1360 and 1370–1388.

[21] Kranz, p. 226. Aeschylus, *Herakleidae* Fr. 109 M has sometimes been taken for dactylo-epitrite, but I have little doubt that Wilamowitz (*Griechische Verskunst,* pp. 460–461) and Wecklein before him were right in thinking that it can convincingly be analyzed in other ways. It certainly does not have the unambiguously dactylo-epitrite character of the two odes in the *PV*.

above (Chapter II 1 *c*). Here I recall and amplify an argument already employed by Thomson (I) : A large proportion of Schmid's *Lieblingswörter*, including many of those that seem to carry the most thematic weight, are already in the process of becoming such in the *Oresteia* (and, I would add, to some extent in the *Su*). This phenomenon therefore behaves remarkably like a number of others, metrical, stylistic, and thematic (see below, Chapter V 5).

Bearing in mind that the *Oresteia* is somewhat over three times as long as *PV*, we see in Table 2 that in almost all these instances (1) the *Lieblingswort* concerned is already tending

TABLE 2

	Su	*Oresteia*	*PV*	*Elsewhere in Aeschylus*
τύραννος and deriv.	0	8 times	13	
(ἐπι-) χαλάω	0	2	6	Once in *Diktyoulkoi**
πημονή	3	2 (3?)	9	Once in *Pe*
πῆμα	1	20	11	*Pe* 6, *Se* 4, Frr. 2
πάσχω	4	16	13†	*Pe* 3, *Se* 5, Frr. 6
τάλας	0	17	6	*Pe* 4, *Se* 7, Frr. 1
νόσος	3	10	10	*Pe* 1, Frr. 2
πόνος	7	23	20	*Pe* 4, *Se* 4, Frr. 11
τορός (-ῶς)	4	10	4	*Pe* 1
εὑρίσκω	6	6	7	*Pe* 3, *Se* 2, Frr. 1
μανθάνω	2	21	12	*Pe* 2, *Se* 2, Frr. 3
τέρμα	1	6	9	Frr. 1

* Schmid might also have noticed Schol. Med. on *PV* 256: συνήθης αὐτῷ ἡ "χαλᾷ" φωνή.

† Not 4, as Schmid states.

to become a *Lieblingswort* in the trilogy, and (2) the tendency is greatly exaggerated in the *Prometheus*. Less certainly, the tendency seems sometimes to be foreshadowed in *Su*.

b) *"Ellipse" of the first and second persons of* εἰμί. Schmid (I, p. 72) stated that *PV* was the only play in the Aeschylean corpus that permitted the "ellipse"[22] of the verb *to be* in the first or second persons. For a long time this struck me as one of his most damaging linguistic arguments against the authenticity of the play. Here was a phenomenon not merely subliminal, but recurring often enough to rule out the possibility of coincidence; Groeneboom (on *PV* 42, cited by Schmid) listed no less than seven examples: 42, 178, 246, 320, 373, 475, and 987.

A careful search of the other Aeschylean plays and fragments, however, convinces me that Schmid was simply mistaken. I may possibly have missed one or two instances still (searching for something that isn't there is a difficult, as well as a peculiar, occupation!), but the following list should be enough to prove the point:

Su 370 σύ τοι πόλις, σὺ δὲ τὸ δήμιον.

πρύτανις ἄκριτος ὤν,

κρατύνεις βωμόν κ.τ.λ.[23]

---

[22] "Ellipse" may not be a strictly suitable term for these cases (cf. Fraenkel, vol. II, pp. 367–368), but I use it for want of a better, and because it is generally recognized.

[23] It seems almost certain, however the passage is punctuated, that the first phrase means "You are the city, you are the people." Just possibly πόλις and τὸ δήμιον could be taken as appositional

Ag 1604 κἀγὼ δίκαιος τοῦδε τοῦ φόνου ῥαφεύς.

Ch 135 κἀγὼ μὲν ἀντίδουλος.

Ch 412 καὶ τότε μὲν δύσελπις (sc. εἰμί).

Eu 578 φόνου δὲ τοῦδ' ἐγὼ καθάρσιος.

Eu 606 ἐγὼ δὲ μητρὸς τῆς ἐμῆς ἐν αἵματι;

The above examples, as far as I know, have not been seriously questioned by editors. The following are slightly more doubtful, but I would, myself, admit them:

Ch 481 κἀγώ, πάτερ, τοιάδε. σοῦ χρείαν ἔχω.

So cod. M. Most editors accept Turnèbe's τοιάνδε, but Murray may be right in keeping the letters given by M, and referring to the similar expression in *Ag* 1360.

Ch 1042–1043 ἐγὼ δ' ἀλήτης τῆσδε γῆς ἀπόξενος,

ζῶν καὶ τεθνηκὼς τάσδε κληδόνας λιπών.

This, the resounding end of Orestes' last long speech in the play, should probably be printed as a complete sentence (so Wilamowitz and Smyth), in which case it will stand as an example of the phenomenon. With less probability, Groeneboom and Murray indicate typographically that the sentence is *interrupted* by the following remarks of the Chorus.

Danaides Fr. 125 M=44 N, line 7 τῶνδ' ἐγὼ παραίτιος.

Not absolutely certain, because this is the last surviving line of the fragment, and a verb could just conceivably have stood in the following line.

---

to the implied subject of κρατύνεις ("As city, as people, you rule"), but I find no editor or translator who does so.

I leave out of account *Eu* 381 ff. (εὐμήχανοι κ.τ.λ.) and *Eu* 780–784 (repeated at 810–814), because in those passages *anacoluthon* is the most likely explanation of the absence of a verb; and *Pe* 909 δύστηνος ἐγὼ στυγερᾶς μοίρας, *Se* 808 οἴ ᾽γὼ τάλαινα, and *Ch* 743 ὦ τάλαιν᾽ ἐγώ, since these are almost certainly to be regarded as exclamations, not statements.

The revised figures for this phenomenon may now be allowed to speak for themselves. They reveal a familiar pattern:

Pe, Se none; *Su* one, plus one (?) from the same trilogy (*Danaides*); *Ag* one; *Ch* two (four?); *Eu* two; *PV* seven.

c) δεῖ. This most familiar and obvious of Greek words made its way rather slowly into Greek poetry. The statistics are similar to those for the resultative perfect (above, 3 *b*).

Homer: once (*Il.* 9.337)

Pindar: once

Aeschylus: not in *Pe, Se*; *Su* four (five?); *Oresteia* fifteen; *PV* four; *Fragments* three (I discount 94 N=141 M, where either χρή or δεῖ may be conjectured).

See Starkie's edition of *Wasps* (London, 1897), on line 1066: "This is a prosaic word, first familiarized in poetry by Euripides (250 times); it occurs . . . 70 times in Sophocles (rare in *OT, OC, Electra,* mostly in *Philoctetes*—22 times)."

d) πέπρωται (*and parts*). Occurrences: not in *Pe, Se, Su*; *Ag* three; *Ch* none; *Eu* one? (conj. for codd. πέπρακται at 125); *PV* six; *P Unbound* one (Fr. 199 N=326 M, line 3); *Fr. Inc. Fab.* one (708 M).

Here is yet another instance of a rather rare feature common to the *Bound* and the fragments of the *Unbound* (see below, Chapter V 6).

  e) *Address formulae.* Schmid (I, pp. 9 and 73–74) and Coman (p. 105) have both commented on the peculiarities of *PV*'s address formulae, referring to Th. Wendel's exhaustive work on this feature in Greek epic and drama. Predictably, Schmid thought they proved the play to be spurious and Coman didn't. Neither, perhaps, digested the results of Miss Wendel's work with enough care. The authoress herself (pp. 64, 138) merely thought that they indicated a later reworking of *PV*. Since her book is not widely accessible, I here restate some of her main points.

  On the whole, Aeschylus is very restrained in his use of address expressions, by comparison with any other epic or dramatic poet.[24] When he does use them, it is with studied effectiveness and—where the more elaborate expressions are concerned—remarkable originality. "In Aeschylus we find nothing schematic. For him an address expression is just a necessary reinforcement of the sense, and it is brought to bear with economy and deliberation. He applies and constructs his address expressions for the individual case" (Wendel, p. 149). This judgment is completely confirmed by the fifty pages of carefully classified instances that make up the first part of her book. If it is granted, however, then clearly we can only use the address formulae as an argument

---

[24] Such expressions occur in the *Iliad* in 4.5% of the total of lines; in the *Odyssey,* 5%; in Sophocles, 6.1%; in Euripides, 6%; but in Aeschylus' work as a whole, only 2.25% (Wendel, p. 53).

against Aeschylean authorship if they prove to be strikingly inept. If they prove to be engineered—like almost every other stylistic detail in an Aeschylean play—to fit the unique content and ethos of the play as a whole, then the lack of parallels need not be damning. Nonetheless, Wendel and Schmid had some reason to be perturbed by the figures shown in Table 3, which I tabulate on the basis of Wendel's material (pp. 5–6), on *address by the proper name alone.*

On a first view these statistics would seem to detach *PV* from any other play of Aeschylus and to range it alongside

TABLE 3

Addresses to:	Aeschylus	Sophocles	Euripides
Gods	*Eu* 1 instance *PV* 1	*Ajax* 1	4 instances in the entire corpus
Men	*Pe* 1 *Ag* 1 *Ch* 2 *PV* 13 (all to Prometheus) Frr. 2	*Ajax* 12 *Ant.* 0 *OT* 7 *Tr.* 2 *El.* 5 *Phil.* 2 *OC* 10	Many instances, e.g., *Cycl.* 14, *Alc.* 11, *Med.* 8
Women	*Ag* 1 (Clytaemn.) *PV* 3 (Io)	*Ant.* 1 *El.* 2 *OC* 2 Frr. 1	Many instances, e.g., *Med.* 8
More than one person	*PV* 1 (Kratos and Bia)	No instances	One instance in the entire corpus

Sophocles' *Ajax* and Euripides' *Cyclops* and *Alcestis*. I would, however, draw attention to two points that do not seem to have been noticed. (1) Of the Aeschylean instances cited from outside *PV*, four are from the *Oresteia*; one (Fr. 190 N=322 M) is from the *Prometheus Unbound,* and is addressed, again, to Prometheus; one (Fr. 227 M) is from the undated *Myrmidons*; one only (*Pe* 713) is certainly from Aeschylus' earlier phase. (2) The very frequent recurrence of a noun in the vocative is not at all unique in Aeschylus. The vocative πάτερ is found six times in *Su,* twelve times in *Ch* (both, it should be noted, plays of the "later group"), but nowhere else in the corpus. Its relevance, and the relevance of its almost narcotic repetition, to those two plays is obvious: Aeschylus would impress on us the roles of Danaos living and of Agamemnon dead. The difference between the artistic use of this common noun in *Su* and *Ch* and of the proper noun *Prometheu* in *PV* does not seem to be great. Further, the significance of the Titan's mere *name* to the theme of this particular play should not be overlooked (cf., especially, lines 85, 505–506). Nor should we forget the complex emotional uses to which the vocative of it is applied: as a sigh by Hephaestus at its first occurrence (line 66), as a sneer by Hermes at its last (951).

I conclude that this feature is no argument for the *PV*'s spuriousness, but yet another instance of what we have seen so often: a bold development of a stylistic device already apparent in the rest of the corpus, above all in the later group. If my reasoning is acceptable, then we need not spend time

over Wendel's further objection (p. 138), that addresses by
a proper name alone do not occur in Aeschylean lyric outside
PV (five instances). Given the small number of other instances, this is not surprising; and we may perhaps add that
πάτερ does occur in lyric, once in *Su* and twice in *Ch*.

Schmid's further observation (I, p. 74), that there are no
parallels to the form of the longer address expressions at *PV*
18, 137–140, 647, 705, need not be taken seriously as an
argument that the play is spurious. Miss Wendel's classified
lists provide many instances of such unparalleled ad hoc crea-
tions from plays other than *PV*; for example, *Se* 39, 203,
792; *Ag* 1295–1296; and *Eu* 1032–1033. Finally, Schmid's
objection that the nominative address ὦ φίλος in *PV* 545–546
stands alone in the Aeschylean corpus has since been met by
the appearance of the same phrase in the *Diktyoulkoi* papyrus
(line 807).

The following two items, (*f*) and (*g*), might just as well
be placed in Chapter Three. In one aspect they are only verbal
repetitions; in another, they might be considered to carry
ideas that are central to the themes of their respective trilogies. I can find no trace, or foreshadowing, of them in *Pe, Se,*
or the Fragments.

f) ἀπαλλαγὴ πόνων, *and related phrases with* ἀπαλλαγή,
ἀπαλλάσσω. For a fuller discussion of this phenomenon, see
Herington (III). Occurrences:

Oresteia: Ag 1=*Ag* 20,[25] *Ag* 335–336, *Eu* 83 (where the

---

[25] For this closely spaced repetition of a key phrase at the opening
of the trilogy, cf. φιλανθρώπου τρόπου in *PV* 11 = 28.

"release from troubles" is no longer prayed for, as it was at the opening of the trilogy, but divinely assured).
PV: 316, 470–471, 749–750, 754, 773 (all with reference to the "release from troubles" of Prometheus or of Io).

There is not even any instance of ἀπαλλαγή or ἀπαλλάσσω with a separative genitive in the special sense "release from" elsewhere in Aeschylus. In *Su,* though the wording does not occur, the *idea* does: *Su*: 802–803 (release from sorrow by death, cf. Io in *PV* 754) and, more significantly, in the Chorus' parting appeal to their mythical prototype, Io, at 1064–1065: ὅσπερ Ἰὼ πημονᾶς ἐλύσατ' εὖ.

g) εὐμενὴς βία (*and related phrases*). This eerie, palintone phrase is heard at the very end of *Su* (1067). The whole passage is worth recalling:

Ζεὺς ἄναξ . . .

. . . ὅσπερ Ἰὼ

πημονᾶς ἐλύσατ' εὖ,

χειρὶ παιωνίᾳ κατασχεθών,

εὐμενῆ βίαν κτίσας.

So far I have found no parallel to it outside Aeschylus, until we reach the Neoplatonists. Thomson (II, on *Ag* 182–183) cites βιαίαν χάριν from Porphyry, and I have noted the phrase *familiari violentia* in St. Augustine's *Confessions* (6.8.1). The *idea* is widespread among Stoic and Christian thinkers; I would cite Seneca *passim* (e.g., *Prov.* 4.7, "Deus quos probat, quos amat, indurat exercet"), and Donne's sonnet *Batter my heart, three-person'd God.*

In Aeschylus similar phrases recur at:

Su 576 (the healing of Io) :

$$\underline{\beta \acute{\iota}\alpha \; \delta', \; \mathring{\alpha}\pi\eta\mu\acute{\alpha}\nu\tau\omega \; \sigma\vartheta\acute{\epsilon}\nu\epsilon\iota}$$
$$\kappa\alpha\grave{\iota} \; \vartheta\epsilon\acute{\iota}\alpha\iota\varsigma \; \mathring{\epsilon}\pi\iota\pi\nu o\acute{\iota}\alpha\iota\varsigma,$$
$$\pi\alpha\acute{\upsilon}\epsilon\tau\alpha\iota.$$

Ag 182: δαιμόνων δέ που χάρις βιαίως . . .

(codd.; malim βίαιος cum Turnebo).

And *PV?* Tentatively I would point out the contrast between the Zeus ἐς τὰ πάνθ' ὁμῶς βίαιος of the dramatic present in that play (lines 736–737)—not to mention his minion Bia on the stage—and the Zeus ἐπαφῶν ἀταρβεῖ χειρί of its prophetic future (line 849). The same idea may well be at work in this trilogy. At least as far as Io and Herakles are concerned, we can still see that *Deus quos probat, quos amat, indurat exercet.*[26]

h) *Metrical statistics.* Compare above, 3 *c* and *d,* for first-foot anapaests and enjambment—both tending to group the *PV* with the *Oresteia.*

Here I add Ceadel's summary statistics on resolution generally in the trimeters of Aeschylus (see also Yorke I). It will at once be seen that they show a steady *decrease* in the frequency of resolution throughout the dated, or approximately dated, plays; with the undated *PV* again ranging itself decisively alongside the *Oresteia.* Aeschylus' trimeter technique in fact became, as far as we can see, increasingly

---

[26] In the prophecies of the *Unbound* it was foretold that Herakles would at last reach the Hesperides, and presumably the apples of immortality: Strabo 4.183 (Fr. 199 N = 326 M).

strict with time.[27] A striking difference between this item
and the other items I have included under (4) is that here
PV only very slightly exaggerates a tendency seen in the
Oresteia; in the other items the exaggeration is violent.

Pe (472 B.C.) : 1 resolution in 8.9 trimeters
Se (467 B.C.) : 1 in 10.4
Su (466 or later) : 1 in 12.1
Ag (458 B.C.) : 1 in 21.6 ⎫
Ch (458 B.C.) : 1 in 18.8 ⎬   Average: 1 in 20.1
Eu (458 B.C.) : 1 in 19.9 ⎭
PV (undated) : 1 in 20.3

As Yorke (I, p. 117) remarks, the figures for the three several plays of the *Oresteia* should reassure us somewhat as to
the validity of this type of statistic. Presumably composed
at nearly the same time for the performance in 458 B.C.,
they show, in spite of their great differences in form and
content, nearly the same frequency in trimeter resolution—
a frequency that sharply distinguishes them from any earlier
dated play of Aeschylus.

We should perhaps see all the more significance in the
fact that the *PV*'s frequency is in the same order of magni-
tude as that of the *Oresteia*, but a fraction lower.

[27] By contrast, Euripides' technique (in this as in some more
important respects) tended toward greater freedom throughout his
traceable career, especially in his last decade—where there is a
rather abrupt acceleration that might be compared (*mutatis mu-
tandis*) to the acceleration in Aeschylus' latest works. In Sophocles'
trimeters, as is well known, no definite trend can be discerned. See
Ceadel for statistics on all three playwrights.

5. *Particles in the* Prometheus

In the original draft of this monograph I submitted the particle usage of *PV* as evidence for its close connection with the *Oresteia*, relying entirely on the judgment of Denniston (p. lxix). At the Toronto seminar, however, Professor H. Musurillo quickly convinced me that that judgment was inadequately based, and that the whole question needed to be examined afresh. The provisional re-examination of which the results are reported here owes much both to Professor Musurillo's suggestions and to the material he generously contributed, but it is still very far from complete. The difficulty of accurately counting and classifying particles and the inevitable unconscious bias to which a mere human being is subject in selecting and presenting the results of such a count suggest that here above all our studies would profit from the discreet application of electronics. Someone—but that someone will not be I!—must attempt a thorough computer analysis of the particles, not only in all Aeschylus but in all fifth-century drama, before the final word can be said. Nevertheless, the following survey may expose a certain number of hard facts bearing on our problem, besides indicating some possible lines of enquiry for others.

I first enumerate the particles that I have checked in Italie, with reference also to the additions in Mette (I, pp. 291–307; II, 234–235). Wherever a particle, or particle usage, or particle combination seemed to show any significant difference between the usage of *PV* on the one hand

and of the remaining six plays on the other, I have added a brief note to that effect. Wherever I have spotted a significant difference between any one Aeschylean play (or small group of plays) and the rest, I have also noted the fact, but this latter set of observations must be taken as incomplete. In counting instances I have, on the whole, accepted all those passages that Italie does not enclose in square brackets.

ἀλλά: The combination ἀλλ᾽ οὖν is found only in *Se* (1 instance) and *PV* (2).

ἄν: The use of this particle *in sentences of command or exhortation* (Italie, s.v., II.5) is distributed thus: *Pe* 0, *Se* 5, *Su* 7, *Ag* 6, *Ch* 5, *Eu* 4, *PV* 0. The combination πρὶν ἄν is found only in *PV* (6 instances) and Fr. 648 M.

ἄρα.

ἆρα.

ἀτάρ: Found only in *Pe* (1 instance) and *PV* (2)

αὖ: Distribution: *Pe* 5, *Se* 3, *Su* 3, *Ag* 4, *Ch* 5, *Eu* 2, *PV* 6, Frr. 2

αὖθις: Distribution: *Pe* 0, *Se* 1, *Su* 0, *Ag* 5, *Ch* 4, *Eu* 2, *PV* 0, Frr. 1

αὖτε: Distribution: *Pe* 1, *Se* 2, *Su* 1, *Ag* 5, *Ch* 3, *Eu* 2, *PV* 0

γάρ: The combination γὰρ οὖν is found only in *Ag* (2 instances), *Eu* (1), *PV* (1), and Fr. 609.5 M (attribution to Aeschylus disputed; cf. Chapter II, n. 12).

γε.

γοῦν: Found only in *Ag* (2 or 3 instances) and in the MSS reading of Fr. 244.2 M δέ: The use of this particle *in anaphora* (Italie s.v., II.7) is distributed thus: *Pe* 4, *Se* 7, *Su* 2, *Ag* 1, *Ch* 3, *Eu* 3, *PV* 0, Frr. 1.

δή.

δῆθεν: Found only in *PV* (2 instances)

δήποτε: Found only in *Ag* (1 instance)

δήπου: Found only in *PV* (1 instance)

δῆτα: The combination οὐ (μὴ) δῆτα is found only in *PV* (3 instances). The combination τί δῆτα is thus disturbed: *Pe* 0, *Se* 0, *Su* 1, *Ag* 2, *Ch* 1, *Eu* 0, *PV* 2, Frr. 1

εἶτα: Found only in *Ag* (2 instances) and *PV* (1)

εἴτε: Distribution: *Pe* 0, *Se* 0, *Su* 1, *Ag* 4, *Ch* 4, *Eu* 3, *PV* 0, Frr. 3

ἔστε: Found only in *Eu* (1 instance) and *PV* (5)

ἤ: Distribution: *Pe* 6 (7?), *Se* 8, *Su* 2 (4?), *Ag* 13 (14?), *Ch* 6 (7?), *Eu* 8, *PV* 13, Frr. 4

ἤ.

ἠδέ: Distribution: *Pe* 12, *Se* 1, *Su* 0, *Ag* 0, *Ch* 2, *Eu* 2, *PV* 0, Frr. 2

θήν: Found only in *PV* (1 instance)

καί: The use *vi adversativa* (Italie s.v., I.3) occurs only in *Su* (1 instance) and *PV* (6). The combination καὶ νῦν is distributed thus: *Pe* 0, *Se* 2, *Su* 1 (where the two words are separated), *Ag* 4, *Ch* 2, *Eu* 4, *PV* 5, Frr. 1.

καίπερ, καὶ . . . περ: Distribution: *Pe* 0, *Se* 1, *Su* 0, *Ag* 1, *Ch* 0, *Eu* 3, *PV* 5, Frr. 1

καίτοι: Found for certain only in *PV* (4 instances); the word is given in the MSS at *Eu* 849, but is usually emended away; it has been restored—but very uncertainly—at Fr. 225.5 M.

μά: Found only in *Ag* (1 instance)

μέν.

μέντοι: Distribution: *Pe* 1, *Se* 3, *Su* 1, *Ag* 4, *Ch* 0, *Eu* 1, *PV* 5, Frr. 1

μή: The combination τὸ μή followed by the infinitive (Italie s.v., IX.4 a,b) is distributed thus: *Pe* 0, *Se* 0, *Su* 0, *Ag* 6, *Ch* 2, *Eu* 5, *PV* 3, Frr. 2.

μηδέ.

μήν: Distribution: *Pe* 5, *Se* 7, *Su* 3, *Ag* 9 (10?), *Ch* 5, *Eu* 4, *PV* 9, Frr. 3

μήτε.

μῶν: Found only in *Su* (1 instance), *Ag* (1), *Ch* (1)

ναί: Found for certain only in *Pe* (3 instances); the word was conjectured by Wilamowitz at *Su* 468.

νῦν, νυν: The combination νῦν δέ in sense "but as things are" is found only in *Ag* (1 instance) and *PV* (2).

ὅπως.

οὐ, οὐκ: *Postponed* οὐ (Italie, s.v. VIII) is cited only once from *Pe* and four times from *PV*. The combination οὐκ ἔστιν ὅπως (ὅστις) is found only in *Ag* (1 instance), *Ch* (1), and *PV* (3).

οὐδέ: The use of this particle *in interrogation* is found for certain in *Eu* (1 instance) and *PV* (3). Two very doubtful instances are cited from *Ag*.

οὔκουν: Found only in *Su* (1 instance), *Eu* (1), and *PV* (5)

οὐκοῦν: Found only in *Se* (2 instances) and *Su* (1)

οὖν: The combination δ᾽ οὖν is distributed thus: *Pe* o, *Se* 1, *Su* o, *Ag* 5, *Ch* 1, *Eu* 2, *PV* 1, Frr. 2.

οὔποτε: Distribution: *Pe* o, *Se* 1, *Su* o, *Ag* 3, *Ch* o, *Eu* 6, *PV* 4, Frr. 2.

οὔτε.

οὐχί: Found only in *Su* (2 instances), *Ag* (1), *PV* (2), Frr. (2). It should be noticed that of the two instances in the Fragments one (Fr. 17.89 M) is certainly from a satyr-play and the other (Fr. 617.1 M) belongs to a group of Aeschylean remarks on *pigs* (χοῖροι) collected by Chamaeleon *apud Athenaeum*, which have a satyric if not downright obscene air.

περ: Distribution (not including instances in which the word is preceded by καί *in tmesi*): *Pe* 1, *Se* 1, *Su* 2, *Ag* 3, *Ch* 1, *Eu* o, *PV* o, Frr. 1

πλήν: Found only in *Ag* (3 instances), *Ch* (1), *Eu* (2), *PV* (8)

που: In local sense, this particle is found only in *Su*, *Ag*, and *Eu* (one instance each). *In other than local senses*, the distribution is: *Pe* 2, *Se* 1, *Su* 1 (2?), *Ag* 3, *Ch* o, *Eu* o, *PV* 5, Frr. 1.

τε: The combination οἷός τε followed by an infinitive in the sense "able to" is found only in *PV* (3 instances).

τοι: The combination τἄρα is found only in *Ch* (2 instances) and in Fr. 710 M. Professor Musurillo has drawn attention to the absence of τοι from the lyrics of *PV*, in contrast to all the other plays of the corpus. His observation is correct, as the following figures show: *Pe*, 9 instances of τοι (of which 4 are in lyrics); *Se* 10 (4 lyric); *Su* 13 (7 lyric); *Ag* 16 (2 lyric, 1 anap.); *Ch* 9 (2 lyric, 1 anap.); *Eu* 9 (2 lyric,[28] 1 anap.); *PV* 8 (0 lyric, 1 anap.). But in view of the relatively low proportion of lyric to dialogue in *PV*, and of the rarity of τοι in lyric already evident in the *Oresteia*, I doubt if any conclusion can be drawn from it— except that, in this as in so many other respects, the *PV* stands nearer to the *Oresteia* than to the other plays.

τοίγαρ: Distribution: *Pe* 3, *Se* 1, *Su* 2, *Ag* 0, *Ch* 1, *Eu* 2, *PV* 0, Frr. 1

τοιγάρτοι: Found only in *Su* (1 instance)

τοίνυν: Found only in *Se, Su, Ch, PV* (once in each)

ὡς: *In consecutive clauses* (Italie, s.v. III. 1,2) distributed thus: *Pe* 4, *Se* 1, *Su* 3, *Ag* 7, *Ch* 1, *Eu* 3, *PV* 0, Frr. 0

ὥσπερ: Distribution: *Pe* 0, *Se* 3, *Su* 0, *Ag* 7, *Ch* 5, *Eu* 2, *PV* 1, Frr. 2

ὡσπερεί: Found only in *Ag* (2 instances) and *Ch* (1)

The information in the above list may be broken down, for our purposes, as follows:

a) *Number of particles employed in each play.* There are fifty-seven items in the preceding list, not counting the sub-headings (i.e., the particle usages and particle combinations). This list shows how many of these items appear, even if only

---

[28] Or 4, if we count the instances in 821 and 823; but these occur in antistrophes that are *verbatim* repetitions of their strophes. I have therefore included only the instances in those strophes, i.e., lines 791 (?) and 840.

once, in the Aeschylean plays severally: *Pe*: 35; *Se*: 39; *Su*: 39; *Ag*: 44; *Ch*: 38; *Eu*: 40; *PV*: 43.

I would not, myself, lay great stress on these figures. A slightly different definition of "particle" might effect considerable changes in them; and further, if we took them strictly as evidence for date, one would be obliged to place the *Choephori* before the *Septem*! Even so, as they stand, they suggest (1) that Aeschylus' *Partikel-Schatz* tended on the whole to increase as time went on, and (2) that *PV*'s *Partikel-Schatz* is proportionately greater than that of any other play in the corpus.

b) *"PV" stands alone among the seven plays.* The following particles, particle combinations, and particle usages are peculiar to *PV*. The number of occurrences in the play is given in parentheses.

δῆθεν	(2)
δήπου	(1)
οὐ (μὴ) δῆτα	(3)
θήν	(1)
καίτοι	(4; I exclude the doubtful instance in *Eu*)
οὔκουν . . . γε	(3)
οἷός τε "am able"	(3)
πρὶν ἄν	(6; also in one fragment)

The following particles or particle usages are *not* found in *PV*, but are found in all the other plays. Reference to our main list, however, will show that in each case there is at least one other Aeschylean play in which the relevant item occurs once only; its total absence from *PV* may therefore perhaps be considered a matter of chance: αὖτε; δέ *in anaphora*; ὡς *in consecutive clauses.*

c) *"PV" shows a noticeably high incidence of a particle (or particle combination or particle usage) in comparison with the other plays.* Here the number of occurrences in *PV* is shown after each item; in parentheses is the number of occurrences in the play(s) with the next highest incidence.

αὖ	6 (*Pe* 5, *Ch* 5)
ἔστε	5 (*Eu* 1; no other occurrence)
ἦ	13 (*Ag* 13, perhaps 14)
καί	*vi adversativa* 6 (*Su* 1; no other occurrence)
καὶ νῦν	5 (*Ag* 4, *Eu* 4)
καίπερ	5 (*Eu* 3)
μέντοι	5 (*Ag* 4)
μήν	9 (*Ag* 9, perhaps 10)
οὔκουν	5 (*Su* 1, *Eu* 1)
που	*in other than local sense,* 5 (*Ag* 3)

d) "PV" sides with plays of the "earlier group" ("Pe," "Se") against the later.

ἀλλ' οὖν: *Se* (1), *PV* (2)

Absence of imperative-hortative use of ἄν : common to *Pe* and *PV*, although occurring at least four times in each of the other plays.

ἀτάρ: *Pe* (1), *PV* (2)

Absence of εἴτε : common to *Pe, Se,* and *PV*; note, however, that the word occurs only once in *Su*.

οὐ *postponed*: *Pe* (1), *PV* (4)

e) *"PV" sides with plays of the "later group" ("Su,"
"Ag," "Ch," "Eu") against the earlier.*

γὰρ οὖν: *Ag* (2), *Eu* (1), *PV* (1)
τί δῆτα: *Su* (1), *Ag* (2), *Ch* (1), *PV* (1)
εἶτα: *Ag* (2), *PV* (1)
ἔστε: *Eu* (1), *PV* (5)
καί *vi adversativa*: *Su* (1), *PV* (6)
τὸ μή: *Ag* (6), *Ch* (2), *Eu* (5), *PV* (3)
νῦν δέ "but as things are": *Ag* (1), *PV* (2)
οὐκ ἔστιν ὅπως (ὅστις): *Ag* (1), *Ch* (1), *PV* (3)
οὐδέ *in interrogation*: *Eu* (1), *PV* (3)
οὔκουν: *Su* (1), *Eu* (1), *PV* (5)
οὐχί: *Su* (2), *Ag* (1), *PV* (2)
πλήν: *Ag* (3), *Ch* (1), *Eu* (2), *PV* (8)

f) *Examples of plays, apart from "PV," which contain
particles not found in the other six.*

Pe: ναί (3 instances)

Ag: γοῦν (2 or 3); δήποτε (1); μά (1)

Ch: τἄρα (2; the word also occurs once in a fragment)
Note that—except for the last instance—this list does not
include particle combinations or particle usages (in contrast
to the list for *PV*, given in *b* above).

g) *Examples of plays, apart from "PV," that show a
noticeably high incidence of a particle (or particle usage),
in comparison with the other six plays.* This list, again, does
not pretend to completeness, especially as regards particle
usages and particle combinations. As in the corresponding

section c (on PV), the number of occurrences in the play(s) with the next highest incidence is added in parentheses to each item.

> Pe: ἠδέ 12 (Ch 2, Eu 2). This striking disproportion—more striking than any shown by PV!—is no doubt due to the epic tone of both particle and play.
>
> Se: δέ in anaphora 7 (Pe 4)
>
> Ag: αὖθις 5 (Ch 4); αὖτε 5 (Ch 4); ὡς in consecutive clauses 7 (Pe 4); ὥσπερ 7 (Ch 5)
>
> Eu: οὔποτε 6 (PV 4)

Conclusion. The somewhat random nature of this class of evidence must be conceded at once. The classical Greek particle, in any hands, is the most delicate of all linguistic phenomena—as mobile, as expressive, as carefully attuned to the emotional situation of the moment as the Italian's gesture or as the latter-day Greek's twitch of his suspenders. In the hands of an Aeschylus there are, a priori, hardly any limits to its versatility. In fact, one would almost predict that an Aeschylean tragedy of eccentric content and tone, such as the *Prometheus*, would show a correspondingly eccentric choice and deployment of particles.

Satisfactory analysis is also made very difficult by the fact that our statistical "population" is usually so restricted in any given instance. The reader may reasonably object that the figures given above under, for example, αὖ, αὖτε, εἴτε, δ' οὖν, and περ are in themselves nonsignificant, because the differences in incidence between play and play are relatively so slight. Under these circumstances our main business must be to see whether any general trends can be discerned. Only here and there will a given particle or usage show such a formidable concentration of instances in one group of plays that we shall feel justified in calling it as an individual witness.

The general picture that I construct from the evidence is as follows. There is a tendency, through Aeschylus' dated plays, for the absolute number of particles employed to increase (list 5 *a*, with the qualifications there made). By that criterion alone, the undated *PV*, which employs more particles than any other play proportionately to its size, and more particles absolutely than any save the *Ag*, should be placed late in the series. This same tendency, to expand the particle resources with time, might account for the relatively large number of particles and usages peculiar to the *PV* (list 5 *b*, which should be compared with the corresponding list for other plays in list 5 *f*). Some of the items in list 5 *b* obviously have little value as evidence for date or authorship; why should the learned be perturbed if *PV* alone shows one or two instances of δῆθεν, δήπου, or θήν, when the *Agamemnon* is alone in using γοῦν, δήποτε, and μά in about the same numbers? Only the four occurrences of καίτοι, and the three of οὔκουν . . . γε and οἷός τε, represent drastic innovations in usage that can hardly be paralleled from the other Aeschylean plays. (The six occurrences of πρὶν ἄν, on the other hand, may be explained simply as proceeding from the unique forward-looking, prophetic atmosphere of this play.)

Section 5 *c* contains ten items in which *PV* shows an unusually high number of instances. It will be noticed that in every item but one ($a\tilde{v}$, where *Pe* and *Ch* tie with five instances) *the runner-up is a member of our postulated "later group" of plays*. In this matter, therefore, the *PV* conforms to the pattern of behavior that we have already observed in this chapter, sections 1 *a*, 3 *b*, 3 *d*, 4 *a*, etc.: it multiplies a feature already current in the later group. The corresponding (but incomplete) list *g*, which contains a few examples of similar behavior in other plays, suggests that the tendency to multiply may already be present in *Ag*.

Finally, lists 5 *d* and 5 *e* should be compared with each other. The former shows five items in which the *PV* sides with *Pe* and/or *Se*; but two of these items are negative, and in none is the statistical "population" of impressive size. On the other hand, list *e* shows no less than twelve items in which *PV* sides with one or more plays of the "later group"; and at least four of these ($\tau\acute{\iota}$ $\delta\hat{\eta}\tau\alpha$, $\tau\grave{o}$ $\mu\acute{\eta}$, $o\dot{v}\kappa$ $\check{\epsilon}\sigma\tau\iota\nu$ $\check{o}\pi\omega\varsigma$, and $\pi\lambda\acute{\eta}\nu$) are impressive individually, either because of their intrinsic nature or because of the number of times they occur in this relatively limited space.

On this evidence alone, incomplete as it is, I would confidently assign *PV* to the later, rather than the earlier, group of Aeschylus' surviving works. Further, the *PV*'s observed tendency to outdo the *Oresteia* in several features would suggest that our play stood at the very end of the series. The eccentricities in *PV*'s particle usage are more pronounced than those observable in any other play of the corpus, but no more so than many of its other stylistic features, great and small. They certainly do not seem enough, in themselves, to justify suspicions of the play's authenticity.

CHAPTER III

Second Criterion: Cosmic View and Trilogic Composition

Several of the considerations presented in this chapter have been argued elsewhere in some detail (in Herington IV; and partly also in V and VI), and are therefore expressed here with somewhat aphoristic brevity. This is certainly not to imply that I think them beyond discussion.

1. Fundamental Difference in Cosmic Background between the Two Groups, Pe–Se and Su–Oresteia–PV

"We observe a sharp break in development between the two oldest works, the *Persae* and the Theban tetralogy, and the three later, the Danaid tetralogy, the *Oresteia,* and the

Prometheia. I am not speaking here of grammatical or metrical minutiae, but of the greatest thing, the universe itself. The difference between the two groups is as fundamental as that. In the *Persae* and the Theban tetralogy there is a simple and stable cosmos, one in which, to put it bluntly, the Divine is united against man: let a human being swerve by a hair's-breadth from the rules, and the Powers of earth and heaven will join together to castigate him. This cosmos, it should be observed, is nearly identical with that found immediately *after* Aeschylus also, in the earlier Sophoclean plays and even in Herodotus; it is the early tragic norm. But in Aeschylus' three later trilogies[1] all is changed. The human and divine cosmos is divided into the enemy camps of male and female, and of the opposites which go with them respectively: light/dark, heaven/earth, new/old; the universal fabric is torn in two. There is a malaise in those last trilogies, more terrifying in its social and religious implications than the worst that Aeschylus can do to us through the medium of the conventional early tragic cosmos in the *Septem.* Though it is true that he does contrive to reunite the world in the *Oresteia* (and no doubt at the end of the other two, fragmentary, late trilogies he contrived the same), yet for the greater part of its course we are witnessing, in Aeschylean terms, an anticipation by more than thirty years of Aristophanes' dialogue between the Just and Unjust arguments, between the old and the new society (see *Clouds* 903–906)."—Herington

[1] I.e., Danaid trilogy, *Oresteia, Prometheia.*

(VI) pp. 80–81; cf. (IV) pp. 388–390 for a more detailed discussion.

2. Trilogic Structure

The Theban trilogy (of which we possess the *last* play) evidently followed the outlines of the traditional saga right through to its terrible end in the mutual killing of the two princes. Aeschylus in fact seems to make that end even more ghastly than do his near contemporaries Pindar and Herodotus, by causing the princes to die childless; so that the trilogy culminates in the disappearance of Laios' male line.[2] The progress is unidirectional—from disaster through disaster to annihilation.

In our other three trilogies the overall rhythm, the relation to the traditional saga, and the finale, all seem to have been quite different. Of course, it is only about the *Oresteia* that we can be certain, and there is always some danger of

---

[2] I do not consider this absolutely certain, but it seems likelier than the alternative view (upheld by Lloyd-Jones, pp. 87–92) that Aeschylus intended the hearers of the *Septem* to think that the slain princes *did* leave children. If he did so intend, he was unusually devious about a point of vital importance to the trilogy then ending: Lloyd-Jones can adduce only three passages, all of them capable of a different interpretation. By contrast *Se* 691 πᾶν τὸ Λαΐου γένος and 813 ἀναλοῖ are not ambiguous at all; and 1056 (whether written by Aeschylus or by a late fifth-century imitator) cannot possibly consist with the assumption that two male infants of Oedipus' line were supposed to be alive and kicking at the end of *this* trilogy. What Aeschylus may have written about the Epigoni in *other* dramatic contexts is irrelevant.

arguing unjustifiably from the known pattern of that trilogy to the pattern of the other two. Yet in the latter the
extant plays combine with the fragments and with circum-
stantial evidence to provide a tolerably strong case for the
following general features.

In the last section we saw that one indisputable common
feature of the three trilogies—one that distinguishes them
not only from *Pe* and *Se,* but from all subsequent ancient
tragedy—is the split in the divine as well as in the human
world. This at once imposes a different overall movement
from that of the Theban trilogy: no longer unidirectional,
but resembling rather the complex movement of a lyric triad,
turn–counterturn–nonresponding epode. In all three trilogies, the antistrophic movement of the first two plays is quite
clear:

> *Su*: attempted crime of the males; *Aegyptioi*: retaliatory
> crime of the females.
> *Ag*: murder of man by woman; *Ch*: murder of woman by
> man.
> *PV*: chaining by the servants of Zeus; *Unbound*: release
> by the son of Zeus.

In the *Prometheia*, indeed—here once again exaggerating a
tendency already visible in the *Oresteia* and possibly in the
Su trilogy—the antithetical balance of the first two plays
appears, from the fragments of the *Unbound*, to have been
worked out with amazing precision.[3]

[3] Ocean scene: Earth scene; Io scenes: Herakles scenes. Ahrens
(quoted by Wecklein II, p. 568), actually thought the likeness

In all three trilogies, the first two plays follow, in broad outline, a narrative that is substantially the same as that found in other versions of the myth at all dates. But in none of the three cases do we find an established myth that covers the events presumably or certainly contained in the *third* play. The universal consensus of the poets and mythographers stops with the murder of the sons of Aegyptus, the vengeance of Orestes, and the release of Prometheus respectively. It would be a reasonable guess in any event that the narrative of the third play was freely composed, either because there was no antecedent traditional myth or, even if one existed, it was unlikely to involve a reconciliation of the flat opposites set up in the two preceding plays. And, in fact, (*a*) the narrative of the *Eumenides,* or the greatest part of it, almost certainly *was* freely composed; (*b*) the only substantial fragment of the *Danaides,* the speech of Aphrodite on the primal marriage of Heaven and Earth,[4] implies a divine and indeed cosmic situation that seems purely Aeschylean and cannot be reconciled even with any of the varying stories in the late mythographers; and (*c*) whatever may have happened in the *Prometheus Pyrphoros,*[5] there is nothing in the later stories

------

between the two plays so great that "si una doctae fuerint tragoediae, taedium non movere non potuerint"! I shall discuss this feature further at the end of Chapter VI.

    [4] Fr. 44 N = 125 M. On the general rhythm of the *Su*-trilogy, Robertson's paper (esp. p. 51) is worth consulting.

    [5] On the *Pyrphoros,* cf. Appendix A.

of Prometheus' fate after his release that seems to provide the plot of a play.

I therefore take it as likely, though not demonstrably certain, that the *Su* trilogy, the *Oresteia*, and the *Prometheus* shared the same unparalleled manner of trilogic composition. The extant *Eumenides*, and the Aphrodite-fragment of the *Danaides*, further make it likely that such trilogic composition involved a reconciling of the opposed forces, and a triumphant finale. See also Herington (IV) pp. 391–394, (V) pp. 113–115.

3. *Influence of Old Comedy*

I have argued elsewhere that many of the most striking features of the *Eumenides* could best be accounted for on the assumption that Aeschylus, experimenting with a new type of tragedy that culminated in joy and hope, was influenced, consciously or not, by the newly developed art of Old Comedy (Herington, V). There, and in IV, pp. 394–396, I also noted a few possible indications of similar influence on the *Su* trilogy and the *Prometheia*.

If any part of that hypothesis is acceptable, then the appearance of apparently comic stylistic features such as those noted above (Chapter II 2 *a, b,* and 3 *b, e*) in the *Prometheus* may become easier to explain.

4. *Appearances of the Gods on Stage*

In the *Su* trilogy (Aphrodite fragment of the *Danaides*)

and the *Oresteia*, gods materialize in the last play of the trilogy. In the former, probably, and certainly in the latter, they appear because the human struggle has reached such proportions that the deities themselves are involved in it. The *Prometheia*, in this as in so many other respects, begins where the *Oresteia* leaves off: Here the divine struggle opens with the opening of the trilogy.

In spite of the general opinion, it may be that Aeschylus did not often introduce gods on the stage. I count only eight plays, outside the three tetralogies under discussion, in which gods can be proved to have appeared,[6] and in only one of those, *Psychostasia*, is there any sign of a clash between deity and deity.[7] Certainly no deity appears in the earlier group of the extant plays, *Pe* and *Se*.

5. *Zeus*

In *Pe* (where, surprisingly enough, he is named five times by the all-Oriental cast) and in *Se* (nineteen times) Zeus is

[6] Of these, one is a satyr-play, *Theoroi*; four have characteristics that have caused some scholars to wonder whether they were not satyric or prosatyric, *Kabeiroi, Oreithyia, Phorkides, Semele* (if Fr. 355 M is rightly assigned to it); two are certainly tragedies, *Psychostasia* and *Phrygians*.

[7] Fragments 203 M (on one reading) and 205 M (the famous tableau of Thetis, Zeus, and Eos) might suggest that this was a three-actor play and therefore belonged to the same late period as the trilogies we are discussing. The *Psychostasia*, also, is the only Aeschylean play apart from *PV* that is recorded in ancient sources to have employed stage machinery (Pollux in Fr. 205f M).

of course a powerful figure, and he often seems almost to be identified with the grim laws of the archaic cosmos. But there is nothing whatever in those two early plays to compare with the intense, critical interest in his personal nature that appears in both the *Su* trilogy (Zeus named forty-five times) and the *Oresteia* (sixty-three times); let alone to compare with the famous hymns in *Su* 86–103, 524–599, and *Ag* 160–183. But I use the word "critical" advisedly. Those who justly admire these great lyric passages have sometimes tended to forget the terrible doubts that accompany them in the same dramas and once even in the same song—the Suppliants' taunts and threats against Zeus in *Su* 144–175, and Zeus's total involvement with the not altogether blameless Olympians in the struggle that runs through the *Eumenides*. (The Furies at the trial score somewhat more than a debating point in 640–643 and 728 when they remind the court how Zeus once bound his own father, and how his mouthpiece Apollo intoxicated the Fates.) It is not a great exaggeration to say that throughout the *Oresteia* (but especially from the opening of *Eu* onward) until its very end one's belief in Zeus's control of the universe, let alone in his just control of it, is held in suspense.

In this matter the *PV* (Zeus named fifty-nine times) clearly ranges itself alongside the *Su* trilogy and the *Oresteia*, and equally clearly is irreconcilable with *Pe* or *Se*. The interest in the nature and function of Zeus has simply become even more impassioned: he has, in fact, moved into the very center of the drama. And the explicit criticism comes at the

beginning (not, as in the *Oresteia,* toward the end), just as
the divine struggle itself comes at the beginning. In this
instance, yet again, the *Prometheia* seems to take the next
logical step beyond the *Oresteia,* to begin where the *Oresteia*
closed.

Here, perhaps, is the place to consider briefly an objection
very commonly raised to the authenticity of the *Prometheus*:
that Zeus appears in so odious a light throughout the play
that Aeschylus cannot possibly have rectified the matter later
in the trilogy. The complete answer to this can, I think, be
expressed in a single sentence. *Suppose that only lines 1
through 396 of the* Eumenides *had been preserved, what
scholar in his senses could or would believe that in the last
third of the same play the "Furies" would have become the
"Kindlies"?* Not only their actions, the noises they make, and
the opinions they express, but also the bestial imagery that is
consistently applied to them, are designed totally to alienate
our sympathies. It is only in the middle third of the play that
these characteristics fade out, and others are merged in,
especially their character of earth-goddesses, powerful for
fertility or the reverse; and only in the last third that their
benign aspect takes entire control.

The *PV* stands to its trilogy in the same ratio as *Eumenides*
1–396 stands to the complete play. It seems reasonable to
conclude that in the *PV* we are witnessing precisely the same
technique on a grander scale; but this time the repulsive
imagery (if so it is to be called) applied to the antagonist is

not bestial, but political. Which is surely a powerful argument *for* authenticity, rather than against it.

6. *Tormented Wanderer*

With the *Su* enters a peculiar motif that I cannot trace either in *Pe*, in *Se*, or in the fragments: the wanderer across the face of the earth, more often than not tormented by a supernatural power.

   a) Io in the *Su*; forming, as it were, a "super-plot" on the lyric and mythic level
   b) The suppliant maidens themselves in the same play
   c) Orestes in *Eu*; in 75–77, 238–240, 249–251, we are told of the enormous tracts of land and sea over which the Furies have pursued him; quite apart from his tormented journey from Argos, to Delphi, to Athens.
   d) Io, of course, recurs in *PV*, this time on the stage; and her wanderings are far longer and more terrible than those alluded to in *Su*.
   e) Herakles in the *Unbound* (Frr. 196, 199–201 N)
The end hoped for by almost all these wanderers, as also by Prometheus himself, is ἀπαλλαγὴ πόνων (cf. Chapter II 4 *f*). And all, in fact, seem to have attained it at last (except for the suppliant maidens, whose fate we simply do not know).

   Housman's celebrated question, "Why should I mention Io? Why indeed?" is perhaps answered by the above list. We can also see why, by a "contamination" of previously distinct legends, she was brought to Prometheus in the Caucasus. Io, otherwise hardly found in serious Greek literature outside some lost works of Hesiod and a dithyramb of Bacchylides (addressed, perhaps significantly, to the Athenians) was the supreme mythical example of a pattern that evidently obsessed the poet in his last years.

7. Conclusion

On both levels, divine and human, there are remarkable parallelisms between the *Su* trilogy, the *Oresteia*, and the *Prometheia*. The divine community, the very universe, is divided against itself; humanity wanders in hopeless and apparently meaningless torment. If there is a hope for "release from troubles," it is, above all, Zeus; but not even Zeus himself can ride above the cosmic storm.

In all these matters, and also in the matter of trilogic composition, the *Prometheia* groups itself with the *Su* trilogy and *Oresteia*, and is sharply distinguished from the plays that we know to be earlier, *Pe* and *Se*. Where the *Prometheia* differs from the *Su* trilogy and *Oresteia*, it differs in degree of intensity, not in kind. Repeatedly in this chapter (as in Chapter II) we have seen how the *Prometheia* progresses a stage or several stages beyond the point at which the *Oresteia* stops.

If I rightly understand these three trilogies as wholes, they are linked together above all by the fact that they are no longer "tragedy" in most ancient, medieval, or modern understandings of that term. For: ἡ μὲν τραγῳδία λύει τὸν βίον, ἡ δὲ κωμῳδία συνίστησιν.[8] In our trilogies we seem to have a new and very transitory art form, one that both destroys and constructs the universe. When we can next pick up the story of Attic tragedy, in the earlier plays of Sophocles, that art form has vanished—and vanished forever from the tragic contests of the Dionysia. The artistic and religious *terribilità* of the elderly Aeschylus did not—perhaps, in the nature of things, could not—retain a Periclean audience for long.

[8] Anon., *De Comoedia* in Kaibel, p. 14. On this question of genre cf. Herington (IV), p. 397.

CHAPTER IV

Miscellaneous Items Perhaps Bearing on Date or Authenticity

Chapters II and III collected the evidence that seemed applicable to my two main criteria: stylistic mannerisms and grand design respectively. Here are a few further points which fall into neither category, but which should be taken into account before we try to reach a general conclusion.

1. *The Third Speaking Part*

Those who accept the theory that Prometheus was represented by a giant puppet[1] are thereby at liberty to suppose

[1] For a recent discussion, and rejection of the theory, see Arnott pp. 96 ff.

that two actors only were required for the *PV*. But they ought
first to account for the following questions: Why there is no
external evidence for such an extraordinary procedure?[2] How
the release of the puppet was convincingly effected in the
Unbound? Why, on the solitary occasion when a giant puppet
was demonstrably used in the Athenian theater, the dramatist went to great lengths to apologize for the puppet's *not
speaking* (Aristophanes, *Peace* 657–664)?

Outsize talking dolls, the data suggest, are not even for
Attic comedians! They are for little girls—and for quite big
Stubengelehrter. If there were in fact *three* speaking parts
in the Prologue,[3] there is a prima facie case for putting the
PV later than *Pe, Se,* and *Su,* and therefore hardly much
earlier than the *Oresteia*—the only other extant work of
Aeschylus for which three speaking actors are certainly
needed.[4]

---

[2] I cannot admit Schol. Med. on *PV* 74 (διὰ τὸ "χώρει κάτω" τὸ
μέγεθος ἐνέφηνε τοῦ δεσμευομένου θεοῦ) as evidence. It reads far
more like a literary man's construction from the text before him than
a record of the way in which *PV* was staged. The scholia include
some *explicit* notes on staging (ad 128, 272, 284, 397), but not
everyone is agreed on the veracity of even these.

[3] One needs only to visualize the play in action to see that, once
the puppet is athetized, three speaking parts are essential: (1)
Kratos, (2) Hephaistos, (3) Prometheus, who, though silent until
line 88, must necessarily have entered with the other two speaking
actors at line 1.

[4] It is not, of course, a certain case. Apart from the problems,
both of authenticity and of staging, presented by the exodus of *Se*
(Lloyd-Jones, pp. 95–96), one must again recall Aeschylus' im-

2. *Dramatic Character of the Prologue (1–87)*

Whatever doubts may be permissible as to the number of
actors in the Prologue, there can be no disputing its dramatic
character. That is preserved in the written text for all to see.[5]
As the actors enter, move about, and converse in relatively
brief interchanges, a living situation and characters are rapid-
ly and economically created *pari passu,* before the spectator's
very eyes. This is utterly unlike the opening of any other
extant Aeschylean play, where either there is no actor-pro-
logue (*Pe, Su*; add the *Unbound,* Fr. 190–191 N, with the
testimony of Procopius), or the situation is expounded in a
monumental solo speech, beginning as a prayer except in *Se.*
Among the fragmentary plays partial parallels for a lively
dialogue at the opening may have existed in the satyric
Diktyoulkoi and in the *Phrygians* (Fr. 243 a M; cf. above,
note on Chapter II 3 *e*). The nearest Aeschylean parallel is
possibly the *second* part of the prologue of *Eu* (64–93,
Apollo and Orestes), where again a situation develops from
cold (as it were) in a dialogue between two actors. But this
does not approach the easy technique of our passage.

For almost exact parallels we have to look to Sophocles.

---

mense versatility in the use of his technical media. The *Su* is now
seen to be an astonishing example, as far as the use of the Chorus
goes; and it is often forgotten that even the *Ag,* for most of its
length, is a *one-actor* play!

[5] Including Ezra Pound: "And I admit the opening of the
Prometheus (Aeschylus') is impressive. (Then the play goes to
pot.)"—*Letters,* p. 94.

The openings of *Ajax, Antigone, Electra, Philoctetes,* and *OC*—five out of the seven extant plays—are handled in just this way. Compare also the following section.

3. *Two Allegedly Sophoclean Features in the* PV *as a Whole*

Recently two observations on the general character of the *PV* have been published that deserve notice here, even if only a brief summary is possible.

a) *The Hero.* Knox (pp. 45–50) remarks, I think justifiably, on the close resemblance between the Aeschylean Prometheus and the Sophoclean hero—especially to the lonely, defiant Philoctetes. After weighing the possibility that Prometheus may have been the model for the Sophoclean hero, Knox finally inclines to the alternative: Aeschylus is here seen to have learned from his younger rival. In that case, as he reasonably argues, the play—if by Aeschylus—must be dated late, *c.* 458–456.

b) *Pity and fear.* Friedrich (pp. 192–195, with note 18 on p. 206) presents a somewhat complex argument, which I hope may be fairly summarized as follows. Lessing's interpretation of Aristotle's "pity and fear" as implying *Mitleid* and *das auf uns selbst bezogene Mitleid*, respectively, seems to apply well to Sophoclean drama (Friedrich notes especially the attitudes of the Choruses in *Trach.* and *Ajax*). It also applies excellently to the *PV*—but to no other play in the Aeschylean corpus. While I personally find Friedrich's argumentation in detail a little too schematic, I believe that he has here put his finger on a striking resemblance in ethos between the *PV* and Sophoclean drama.

4. *The Monodies*

The actor-monodies in *PV* 114–117 (or –119) and 566–608, not in lyric interchange with the Chorus, are unique in Aeschylus. Such monodies are fairly frequent in post-Aeschylean tragedy, especially Euripidean: The passages are collected by Owen, 149–152. I would add that the closest formal parallels to Io's monody (long strophe–four trimeters spoken by the calmer Prometheus–antistrophe) that I have noticed are as follows:

Soph. *Ajax* 394–427 (long strophe by Ajax–2 trimeters by Tecmessa–antistrophe by Ajax)

Eur. *Alcestis* 393–415 (strophe by child–2 trimeters by Admetus–antistrophe by child)

Eur. *Andromache* 1173–1196 (strophe by Peleus–2 trimeters by Chorus–antistrophe by Peleus)

Eur. *Supplices* 990–1030 (long strophe by Evadne–3 trimeters by Chorus–antistrophe by Evadne)

But none of these passages is preceded, as the *PV* passage is, by astrophic monody.

5. *Pre-Socratic Echoes in* Su *Trilogy,* Oresteia, *and* PV

Passages in Aeschylus that apparently betray the poet's awareness of contemporary or earlier philosophical thought have been noticed for a very long time. Perhaps it is worth quoting two early scholars (both of them exceptionally well qualified to judge) by way of preface to this section.

"Σημείωσαι. Apparet in multis Aeschylum non fuisse ἀμύητον librorum philosophorum quorum dogmata et sententias saepe perstringit."—Casaubon.

"Pollet etiam [Aeschylus] tacita quadam, Pythagoricae affini, sapientia."—Thomas Stanley.[6]

What has not, I think, been sufficiently noticed is the fact that all the probable instances occur in the *Su* trilogy, *Oresteia,* and *Prometheia* and in a fragment of an uncertain play.[7] Here is the list:

> *Su,* 96 ff., cf. 595 ff. (the motionless God): cf. Xenophanes B 25, B 26, with Kirk and Raven's comments on these fragments; and Fiori-Sole's article.
>
> *Su,* 559 (the Nile floods): cf. Anaxagoras A 42, A 91;

---

[6] Casaubon's marginal note on *PV* 887 ff., quoted by Fraenkel (vol. I, p. 65); Stanley's epistle dedicatory to his edition of 1663.

[7] Two other fragments may be mentioned here, though with some hesitation. (*a*) Fr. 667 M = 390 N ὁ χρήσιμ' εἰδώς, οὐχ ὁ πόλλ' εἰδώς, σοφός is rather like Heraclitus' famous πολυμαθίη νόον οὐ διδάσκει κ.τ.λ. (Heracl. B 40), but not like enough for us to be sure that Aeschylus is echoing the thought of the philosopher. (*b*) 730 M = 457 N, as it stands, ranks Aeschylus with οἱ φυσικώτεροι because he somewhere implied that the moon's light is a reflection from the sun (cf., e.g., Anaxagoras B 18). But Nauck, ad loc., shows some reason for thinking that the author of this statement really meant to say "Euripides," not "Aeschylus."

Vürtheim, p. 74 f. The same theory seems to be implied in:

Fr. Inc. Fab 300 N=193 M (Mette attributes to *Memnon*, on insufficient grounds).

Danaides, Fr. 44 N=125 M (the Aphrodite speech): cf., perhaps, Empedocles B 73, and Anaxagoras A 112 (adding Vitruvius VIII praef. 1, which D-K neglect).

Eumenides, 658 ff. (Apollo's "biology"): this seems a clear allusion to a problem under discussion by half a dozen philosophers and medical men in the middle years of the fifth century. See references collected in Herington (VI) p. 81 n. 31.

Prometheus, 88 ff.: allusion to a four-elements theory (this allusion is already recognized in Schol. Med.)— perhaps Empedoclean? Cf. *Phoenix* 17 (1963) 192–195.

Prometheus, 459–460 (the excellence of Number): a Pythagorean notion; see the references collected by Thomson (I) on his lines 475–476.

6. *Sophistic/Rhetorical Echoes in the* Prometheus

Schmid I (*passim,* and especially pp. 75, 95ff.) makes an excellent case for sophistic/rhetorical influence on the *PV.* On almost all points, except for his final interpretation of the phenomena, I agree with him. The emphasis, which he observed, on σοφός and derivatives (especially the apparently pejorative use of σοφιστής, 62, 944), τέχνη, πόρος, ὠφελέω and derivatives,[8] εὐβουλία, δυοῖν θάτερον—all these seem to point unambiguously in that direction.

On one point Schmid should be corrected. The emphasis on πειθώ as a substitute for βία is no doubt a sophistic/ rhetorical trait in the *PV* (Schmid I, p. 94), but Schmid should have observed that it is also central to the *Eu* (e.g., 5, 970 ff.), and perhaps can be observed already in *Su* 621– 624 (Pelasgos' speech sways the Argive *demos*; here, unless I am mistaken, we actually find a rhetorical term, στροφή, in line 623). I would suggest that this trait, far from indicating the spuriousness of the *PV*, is another proof of its close relationship to the *Su* trilogy and the *Oresteia*.

Three tentative additions may also be made to Schmid's list:

a) *PV* 266 ἑκὼν ἑκὼν ἥμαρτον. Personally I find it difficult not to connect this astonishing phrase with the debate on the paradox "Virtue is Knowledge," which, as Snell (his chapters III–IV) reasonably suggests, can be traced also in some Euripidean tragedies from the *Medea* of 431 B.C. on- ward.

b) As far as I know it has not been observed that the pejorative use of ἀρχαῖος, which occurs quite casually in Ocean's speech at line 317, appears here for the first time in Greek literature and does not reappear until the last third of the fifth century. This special meaning ("out of date" or

[8] These were further examined, with similar results, in Skard's article.

"silly," instead of the normal "ancient" or "august") must surely have originated among radical thinkers; it implies a view of society and history quite alien to the archaic world, and indeed unusual in the ancient world generally. Not surprisingly, most of the other fifth-century instances appear in a radical or sophistic context. To enumerate them all would take too long, but I would note Ar. *Wasps* 1336 (the earliest datable instance), *Clouds* 915 and 984 (the Adikos Logos), 1357, 1469 (the newly "sophisticated" Pheidippides), Euripides Fr. 1088, and Thuc. 1.71.2, 7.69.2 (both in compounds).

c) The antithesis λόγῳ / ἔργῳ, *PV* 336 and 1080. Schmid (I, p. 56) collects certain pre-Aeschylean and Aeschylean parallels, but fails to notice that those refer only to the contrast between the two different sides of human activity, speech and action (e.g., *Il.* 9.443), or between myth and verifiable fact. But the contrast in the *PV* is the far more sophisticated contrast between Word and Reality, which (it is not too much to say) obsessed the Athenians from Euripides through Thucydides to Plato. The earliest non-Aeschylean parallels in this sense known to me are Anaxagoras B 7, Herodotus 3.72, and Cratinus Fr. 300. Possible Aeschylean forerunners are *Se* 847 (οὐ λόγῳ) and *Su* 598 (ἔργον ὡς ἔπος).

Note on Items 5 and 6: To me the passages collected here, scattered though they are, constitute proof that Aeschylus was fully aware of contemporary advanced thought during the years from the production of the *Su* (not earlier than 466 B.C.) onward. I have speculated elsewhere (IV, pp. 388, 396–397; VI, pp. 80–81) as to whether this awareness of the approach of a new intellectual and social era may not have actually conditioned the ideas and the shape of the dramas produced during his last phase. We do not know enough to be positive, but this is the most likely way I know of accounting for the difference in style and implied cosmos between the earlier and later groups of his surviving tragedies.

CHAPTER V

Résumé of the Results of Chapters II, III, and IV

1. *Unparalleled Features of the "PV"*

Chorus' iambic utterances almost entirely limited to quatrains (II 1 *a*)

Formal pattern in line arrangement (II 1 *b*)

High frequency of word and phrase repetition (II 1 *c*)

2. *Features of the "PV" Paralleled in Comedy, but Not in Tragedy*

Certainly: High incidence of nonstop interlinear hiatus (II 2 *b*)

Doubtfully: Initial *rho* not making position (II 2 *a*); high incidence of first-foot anapaests (II 3 *c*)

3. *Features of the "PV" Paralleled Closely in Sophocles*
Enjambment (II 3 *d*)
1:2 Stichomythia (II 3 *e: Ajax*)
Dactylo-epitrite meter (II 3 *g*; in *Ajax,* etc., also in Euripides)
Character of the Prologue (IV 2)
Hero-type (IV 3 *a*)
"Pity and fear" (IV 3 *b*)
Monodies (IV 4: nearest parallel, chronologically, seems to be in *Ajax*; but cf. also, below, 4)

4. *Features of the "PV" Paralleled Closely in Euripides*
High proportion of resultative perfects? (II 3 *b*)
Address formulae? (*Cyclops,* II 4 *e*; but see qualifications there)
Monodies (IV 4: parallels in *Alc., Androm., Suppl.*; but cf. also above, 3)
The sophistic/rhetorical element in the *PV* (IV 6) can also be paralleled in Euripides, *passim*

5. *Features of the "PV" Paralleled or Foreshadowed in the Aeschylean Corpus*

It seems that the simplest and most helpful way of summarizing this information is in the form of a table—at much sacrifice, I fear, of precision. The reader is urged to refer back constantly to the sections in which the phenomena are discussed.

An asterisk means that the feature in question occurs in the play. Unless otherwise stated in the margin, numerals simply represent the absolute number of occurrences of the feature in question. The entries under *"Su"* and *"PV,"* from the item "split universe" onward, may embrace the trilogies to which those plays belonged as well as the plays themselves.

TABLE 4

Date:	*Pe* 472 B.C.	*Se* 467 B.C.	*Su* not earlier than 466 B.C.	*Oresteia* 458 B.C.	*PV* ?
Total no. of lines:	1077	1078	1073	3796	1093
No. of trimeters:	429	515	400	2104	773
Ratio of resolutions to no. of trimeters (II 4 *b*)	1:8.9	1:10.4	1:12.1	1:20.1	1:20.3
First-foot anapaests (II 3 *c*)	2	2	2	11	12
Enjambments (II 3 *d*, end)	1	0	1	8 (7?)	21
Choric quatrains (II 1 *a*)	0	0	1	10	9
Resultative perfects (II 3 *b*)	0	2	1	3	5
Ellipse of 1st and 2nd persons of εἰμί (II 4 *b*)	0	0	1	5 (7?)	7
δεῖ (II 4 *c*)	0	0	4 (5?)	13	4
πέπρωται etc. (II 4 *d*)	0	0	0	3 (4?)	6
Address by simple proper name (II 4 *e*)	1	0	0	4	16

ἀπαλλαγὴ πόνων, etc. (II 4 f)	o	o	(similar phrases)	4	5
Split universe (III 1)	—	—	* (?)	*	*
"Triadic" trilogy structure (III 2)	N/A	—	* (?)	*	*
Appearances of gods on stage (III 4)	—	—	*	*	*
Number of mentions of Zeus by name (III 5)	5[1]	19	45	63	59
Zeus under question (III 5)	—	—	*	*	*
"Tormented wanderer" (III 6)	—	—	*	*	*
Io (III 6)	—	—	*	—	*
Third actor (IV 1)	—	— (?)	—	*	*
Pre-Socratic echoes (IV 5)	—	—	4	1	2
Sophistic/rhetorical echoes (IV 6)	—	—	* (??)	* (??)	*

6. *Rare or Unique Features Shared by the "PV" and the Fragments of the "Unbound"*

High frequency of word and phrase repetition (II 1 c, fin.)

Two-syllable overlap in anapaestic dimeters (II 3 f)

πέπρωται (II 4 d)

[1] We should remind ourselves, once more, that all the speakers in this play are Persians!

Address by simple proper name (II 4 e)

First-foot anapaest in *Unbound,* Fr. 326.7 M (II 3 c); this
occurrence is fairly striking, since only, at most, twenty-
three trimeters survive from the play.[2]

Tentatively, we may perhaps add the numerous mentions
of Zeus by name (III 5); there are six in the fragments of the *Unbound.*

---

[2] This total includes Fragments 194, 195, and 198 Nauck (336,
327, 328 Mette), none of which is attributed specifically to the
Unbound in our sources. Without them, the total is only 16 trimeters.

CHAPTER VI

Some Conclusions

To me one certain conclusion, at least, emerges from the above survey: *If the "PV" is by Aeschylus, it must belong to his later phase.* By both my major criteria (above, Chapters II and III), where the play finds parallels in Aeschylus at all, it finds them in the *Su* or *Oresteia*, not in the *Pe* or *Se*. The miscellaneous items collected in Chapter IV (especially sections 1 and 5) point in the same direction.

A second conclusion is almost equally certain. *The "PV," whoever its author may have been, was probably written after the "Oresteia."* A remarkable pattern has recurred in our data of all types: a mere tendency observable for the first time in the *Su* or *Oresteia* or both (but most often in the *Oresteia*) is developed with great violence in the *Prome-*

theus. The more I review the phenomena summarized in
Table 4 (Chapter V 5) the less likely does it seem to me that
the order can possibly have been *Prometheus–Oresteia.* In
almost all respects, from its theology through its general design down to the humblest details of language and metrics,
the *Prometheia* takes a long stride beyond the *Oresteia.*
Perhaps the only striking exception to this rule is afforded
by the general statistics on trimeter resolution (Chapter II
4 *b*). Yet even though they display no violent exaggeration
in the *Prometheus'* practice, they still seem to place the
Prometheus (to say the least) no earlier than the *Oresteia,*
and at a very considerable remove from the *Oresteia's* nearest predecessor, the *Supplices.*

For these reasons I should be absolutely confident in dating
the *PV* not earlier than 466 B.C. (the earliest possible date
for the *Su*), and little less so in dating it after the production of the *Oresteia* in 458. They seem to me to outweigh the
scanty arguments, most of them based on external grounds,
which have been alleged in favor of a date around 470 B.C.,
during Aeschylus' visit to Sicily at the invitation of Hieron.[1]

The survey proves to be decisive on the question of date.
Is it less so on the question of authenticity?

There are, theoretically, three choices before us. Either
the *PV* was composed by Aeschylus; or it was not composed

---

[1] The latter has been the preferred date of a number of eminent
scholars, from Wilamowitz onward. For a brief consideration of
their main reasons, see Appendix B.

by him but by some person unknown;[2] or, thirdly, we might account for the phenomena by supposing that it was composed partly by Aeschylus and partly by an unknown, being a case either of collaboration or of revision.

The third choice may be ruled out at once. If any of the phenomena that have really perplexed students of the *Prometheus* were confined to certain areas or elements of the play exclusively, then it might deserve serious consideration. But in fact those phenomena are either inherent in the grand design of the play (e.g., the apparent disparagement of Zeus, and the character of Prometheus), or more or less evenly distributed through its entire length (e.g., the repetitions, the nonstop interlinear hiatuses, the enjambments). Deny them to Aeschylus, and you have denied the *Prometheus* to him; for all practical purposes you have adopted the second choice.[3]

[2] For I presume that no one will propose any of the other *extant* dramatists as the author?

[3] There exists, of course, testimony to the effect that some of Aeschylus' plays were revised after his death, but less of it than is often assumed. It is confined to a single passage in Quintilian, 10.1.66. This testimony should not be confused with the evidence to the effect that Aeschylus' plays were *restaged* after his death (*Vita Aeschyli* 12, Ps.-Plut. *Vitae X Oratorum* 841 e, *Suda* s.v. *Euphorion*).

I may here mention *honoris causa*, but without enthusiasm, two proposals to excise specific parts of the *Prometheus*. Schmid (I, pp. 5–16) was inclined to athetize the Ocean scene, wholly or partially; and Kranz (pp. 226–228) denied Aeschylus' authorship of the second and third stasima. To me neither proposal is sup-

Either, therefore, the *Prometheus* is by Aeschylus, or it is
by an unknown. "Look here, upon this picture, and on this!"

If it is by an unknown, then its history must have run as
follows:

"A dramatist who is no longer identifiable composed the
Prometheus Bound and the *Prometheus Unbound*[4] at some
time between *c.* 458 and *c.* 441 [for the latter approximate
date, see Appendix B]. His work and, presumably, he himself at once acquired a fame that endured in Athens for over
a century. Sophocles and Euripides show many traces of his
influence; Aristophanes parodies the *PV* in the *Knights* of
424 B.C., the *PV* and possibly the whole trilogy in the *Birds*
of 414; and he is still at it in the *Ploutos* of 388. The *PV*
is certainly known to Plato.[5] Nevertheless, by the time the
Prometheus-Master's work reached the Alexandrian Library
its author's name had been entirely forgotten. Nay, worse:
the name of Aeschylus had been craftily substituted for it.
It happens that we can date this wretched event within quite

---

ported by convincing arguments, but, even if both scholars were
allowed to have their way, the general problem would remain
exactly where it was before.

[4] The evidence summarized in Chapter V 6 makes it virtually
certain that the two plays must stand or fall together. Schmid's
attempt to dissociate the two, in any case, leads him into a slough
of improbable, not to say frantic, hypotheses (Schmid I, pp. 97 ff;
to me, the weakest part of his book).

[5] Most of these allusions are collected by Schmid (I) and Niedzballa. For the parallels in Plato, see Keseling; for those in the
Ploutos, see Herington in *Phoenix* 17 (1963) 237 n. 9.

narrow limits. It must have occurred almost certainly after the lifetimes of the four great fifth-century dramatists (who surely knew the real author's name) and quite certainly before the constitution of an official text of the three great tragedians on the proposal of Lycurgus in 330 B.C. This text later reached Alexandria, and presumably already contained the *Prometheuses* under the name of Aeschylus—or surely the Alexandrians would have suspected the truth! And all this took place without a murmur of objection from Aeschylus' family, although its most distinguished member (after Aeschylus himself), the tragedian Astydamas II, was active in the theater until at least 340 B.C.

"Worse yet: The Alexandrians did not even follow their usual practice of checking the didascalic records to see whether or not the *Prometheuses* were entered there (and, if entered, whether under Aeschylus' name). They catalogued the plays as Aeschylean without further ado, and crowned their pompous impudence by composing commentaries on them in which they enforced their views by appeals to Aeschylus' συνήθεια. Seldom has a dramatist of the Prometheus-Master's stature been so scurvily served by scholars—and never, as far as our knowledge goes, were the drama specialists of the Library so negligent of their duty. Still, the ingenuity of the new scholarship has at last unmasked the effrontery of the old. The artistic personality, though not (alas!) the name, of the Prometheus-Master can now to some extent be recovered. He is, it must be confessed, uncannily like Aeschylus. Alone among all the Attic tragedians known to us, he followed the older poet's short-lived example in composing a kind of cosmic meta-tragedy. He shared Aeschylus' obsession with the very rare myths of Io and Prometheus.[6] He even continued, and exaggerated, numerous stylistic and metrical tendencies that we can trace in the two latest genuine works of Aeschylus; and at the same time he was no more shy than Aeschylus himself was of taking a hint or two from Sophocles. No doubt because it was his fate to appear in the contests later than either of those great tragedians, the Prometheus-Master contributed but little to the development of the tragic art. Nevertheless, we credit to him the introduction of heavy machinery to the stage [*Footnote*: Pollux's reference to such machinery in the indisputably Aeschylean *Psychostasia,* Fr. 205 M, cannot be taken seriously]; the bold abandonment of the tragic restriction on nonstop interlinear hiatus, and, of course, the *Prometheus Bound.* It is, on the whole, to be regretted that nothing of his other work survives."

That is one of our only two possible alternatives. Ὅστις τοιαῦτ' ἔχει ἐν ἡδονῇ, ἐν ἡδονῇ ἔχει τοιαῦτα—as the Muse of History says in Max Beerbohm.

The difficulties in the way of our other alternative, that

[6] Prometheus is found in the "genuine" Aeschylus in the satyr-play of the *Pe* tetralogy; the *Sphinx* (Fr. 235 N = 181 M); and possibly in *Se* 432–433. (It seems at least possible that the naked torch bearer on Capaneus' shield there is the same person as the naked torch bearer identified as "Titan Prometheus" on Tydeus' shield in Eur. *Phoen.* 1121–1122.)

the play is by Aeschylus, remain grave; but not as grave as Schmid supposed.

Rereading Schmid and others of his generation (e.g., Farnell), I sense that the prime motive for their doubts about the *PV* is highly emotional—though perfectly understandable if one considers the sub-Victorian religious and literary climate in which they had matured. It was a generation when (to put it briefly) permanence was still thinkable, at all levels of the universe. A *mobile* concept of deity, an incontestably great poet who was still navigating the abysses of the cosmos in his sixties, were not thinkable. Hence they inevitably misread our only trilogy, the *Oresteia.* From its opening and closing choruses they collected the comforting message that Zeus was . . . fundamentally sound. What they could not assimilate (however alert they were to other aspects of that infinitely complex work) were the appalling tensions between; the moments when right does not seem in any way distinguishable from wrong; the period in the *Eumenides* when the new gods, including Zeus, stand embattled against the old. Their opinion was reinforced by two accidents. Only the first play of the *Danaid* trilogy had survived, and from about the era of the publication of *The Origin of Species*[7] that play had been almost universally dated to the beginning of Aeschylus' career. It was therefore fatally easy, once more, to accept the majestic intuitive visions of Zeus in the choruses of the *Supplices* as definitive statements and to forget that in

[7] But no earlier! Boeckh and others of his generation dated *Su* to 461 B.C.

the succeeding play those same protégées of Zeus would almost certainly be guilty of stealthy massacre. At the same time, another conclusion imposed itself: from the 490's until at least 458 Aeschylus consistently proclaimed a concept of Zeus that far transcended the ordinary mythological Zeus of his day, and in some ways even approached Jewish/Christian notions of deity. (The cruel archaic cosmos of the supposedly intervening *Pe* and *Se* was for some reason ignored.)

Granted that construction, and granted also a failure to notice the astonishing shifts in perspective and imagery that, in the course of the still-extant *Eumenides,* transform blood-gorged demons into gentle earth powers,[8] then the *Prometheus Bound* must necessarily seem like an obscene word scrawled across the religious experience of a great poet's lifetime. The generous impulse to athetize becomes understandable, even admirable. I now submit, however, that the redating of the *Supplices,* together with an impartial rereading of the *Oresteia* and a reasonably firm dating of the *Prometheia* in the same late phase, simply deletes the construction that gave rise to that impulse. We retain (I believe) the transcendent concept of Zeus, but we now see that that concept was not so quickly or so simply arrived at as our fathers supposed, either in the trilogies or in the poet's life.

Thus, I think, the central difficulty has quietly vanished. The difficulties that remain, though still serious, are not of the same order. I see them as follows:

[8] Above, Chapter III 5, *fin.*

a) The apparently "Sophoclean" character of the Prologue and even, according to some good judges, of the entire play

b) The strong sophistic/rhetorical cast of the language and thought

c) The violent acceleration of change in metrical and stylistic practice, seen in the first half of Table 4 (Chapter V 5) and, for example, in the list of *Lieblingswörter* in Chapter II 4 *a*. I do not see here a complete break with previous practice, but I admit that there is acceleration on a scale that is hard to account for, especially if the *PV* is to be dated (as the evidence strongly suggests) within the short space of two years between the *Oresteia* and the poet's death.[9]

d) Initial *rho* and nonstop hiatus (Chapter III 2 *a, b*)

e) Unparalleled formal regularity (Chapter II 1 *a, b*, cf. Chapter II 3 *e*)

I must confess that even if no explanation whatever were available for these features, I should still be confident in attributing the *Prometheus* to Aeschylus. They do not seem heavy enough to outweigh the undoubtedly Aeschylean (and, above all, late-Aeschylean) features that have, I hope, become clear from the preceding discussion. But in fact an explanation is available. It is, indeed, speculative—as any explanation of so delicate a thing as style ultimately must be. The investigation has reached a point where the hard facts are beginning to give out, and τὸ εἰκός is becoming our only

[9] Note, however, that the difficulties in the way of supposing such an acceleration to have occurred *before* the *Oresteia* are infinitely greater.

resource. But it is at least worth pausing to consider whether the unusual circumstances of the poet's last years may not be responsible, in part, for the unusual character of his last work.

Focke (esp. pp. 298–304), following hints by Wilamowitz and Körte, developed in detail a theory that the stylistic and other peculiarities of the *PV* could be accounted for on the simple supposition that it was written in Sicily.[10] On the grounds, primarily, that Snell had shown that the *Handlung* of the *PV* was more primitive than that of the *Oresteia*, Focke (pp. 261 ff.) opted for a date *c.* 470 as most appropriate for the composition of the play; that is, during Aeschylus' visit to Sicily on the invitation of Hieron, which must have fallen between (at the outside) spring 472 and spring 467 B.C.[11]

Snell's book[12] was hot from the press at the time when Focke wrote, so the latter may be excused for being carried away by a treatment that, at this distance of time, may appear a little schematic, a little too inclined to assume that the ancient lyric dramatist was composing in full awareness of the modern scholar's *Problem*. To me the dating *c.* 470 is

[10] The lines on the Etna eruption (*PV* 366–372) had, of course, long been adduced as evidence that the play was written during one or other of Aeschylus' Sicilian residences. The great merit of Focke, and of the other two scholars named, was their realization that a visit to *the Sicily of that era* might have had profounder effects on an intelligent Athenian than a passing interest in vulcanology.

[11] Herington (VI), pp. 75–76. VI also contains an examination of the detailed evidence for Aeschylus' visits to Sicily, generally.

[12] *Aischylos und das Handeln im Drama*, Philologus Suppl. 20 (1928). Pp. 96–111 concern the *PV*.

convincing neither on Snell's ground, nor in view of all the evidence assembled in our present discussion, nor even on Focke's own terms. For Focke supposed that the *Bound* and *Unbound* constituted a *dilogy* (he denied that the *Pyrphoros* had any connection with them), written to be performed in Sicily, not in Athens. To this a single objection is perhaps decisive. In *c.* 470 Sicily was governed almost entirely by tyrants, of whom the greatest was Aeschylus' host, Hieron. How long would the latter (or his infamous agents, the δορυφόροι, the ὠτακουσταί, the ποταγωγίδες) have sat motionless through a performance of the *PV*, that most subtle study in the behavior and psychology of despotism ever composed? I doubt if a production of the dilogy would have lasted until the interval![13]

If, on the other hand, we transfer the composition of the *PV* to Aeschylus' final residence in Sicily (458–456/5 B.C.), then we shall not only meet this political objection,[14] but we

[13] Incidentally, the Syracusan ποταγωγίδες (Aristotle, *Pol.* 1313 b) are the only female police agents known to me from the fifth century B.C., apart from the comic Skythaina in *Lysistrata* 184, and the far-from-comic Bia, Zeus' policewoman in *PV*.

[14] By the time of Aeschylus' last residence, Sicily was almost entirely under democratic government (Méautis, pp. 67 ff.). For my own purposes this is not an important point, since I see no reason to adopt Focke's assumption that the *PV* must have been composed for a Sicilian theater. I am equally ready to believe that the *Prometheia* was composed with an Athenian performance in mind; after all, Aeschylus could not know that his latest residence in Sicily was doomed to last forever! It could then have been among the unperformed works with which Euphorion II "won four vic-

shall also satisfy the requirements of the stylistic and thematic evidence collected above. And Focke's theory, in general, will work as well as it did before, or better.

A prolonged residence in Sicily after the composition of the *Oresteia* could in itself explain the abrupt jolt forward—rather than break—in the thought and style of Aeschylus, which has so surprised us in the *Prometheus*. At that time Sicily was still the home of the philosopher-poet Empedocles, and of the sophisticated and realistic comedy developed by Epicharmus; but (most interesting in the present context) the rhetoricians Corax and Tisias and the young sophist/rhetorician Gorgias were now also at work in it. I would stress that, according to Cicero,[15] Corax and Tisias wrote the earliest *Art of Rhetoric* known to antiquity "cum sublatis in Sicilia tyrannis res privatae longo intervallo iudiciis repeterentur," that is, some time in the years following 466 B.C.[16] Their activity therefore coincided almost exactly with our postulated "last phase" of Aeschylus' career and must have overlapped with his final Sicilian residence of 458–456. In that way the new sophistic/rhetorical influence that is so apparent in *PV* becomes immediately intelligible. The Sicily of that date—but not of any earlier period in which Aeschylus is known or conjectured to have visited there—was in this

---

tories" (presumably at Athens) after his father's death; according to the *Suda,* s.v. *Euphorion.*

[15] *Brutus* 46.

[16] If we may trust, at least within a year or so, the date given for the collapse of the Sicilian tyrannies by Diodorus, XI. 68.

respect, as in others, far in advance of Athens. We need only recall the impression made at Athens by the arrival there of the elderly Gorgias in 427 B.C., almost exactly a generation later than Aeschylus' death![17]

It is possible—I will not say more than possible—that our difficulties (a), (c), and (d) can be partly accounted for on the same assumption, as follows. Epicharmus certainly knew Aeschylus' work well enough to anticipate Schmid; for Epicharmus also is reported to have made fun of the tragedian for overusing a *Lieblingswort,* τιμαλφεῖν.[18] The Epicharman comedy titles *Persai, Thearoi,* and *Promatheus or Pyrrha,* have also been adduced, probably rightly, as evidence to the same effect. That Epicharmus should have shared Aeschylus' interest in the very unusual dramatic theme of Prometheus can, in fact, hardly be coincidence.[19] The possibility, therefore, cannot be excluded that Aeschylus was in a position to be equally familiar with Epicharmus' style, and was consciously or unconsciously affected by it.

In fact the fragments of Epicharmus' trimeter verse, as far as they go, lend some support to this possibility. The

---

[17] On this question as a whole, cf. Herington (VI), p. 74.

[18] Schol. Med. ad *Eu* 626 (in the extant Aeschylus the pompous word occurs four times—all in the *Oresteia*).

[19] For the new papyrus fragments of the *Promatheus,* cf. P. Oxy. 25 (1959). Unfortunately they were too badly preserved to provide any reliable data for the table of statistics given in my text just below. The idea of a connection between Epicharmus and Aeschylus is, of course, far from new; references are collected in Bock, pp. 417, 439. Cf., in particular, Körte, p. 213, Focke, p. 302.

following figures, based on the Epicharman fragments as
printed in Kaibel, should be compared with the figures for
the corresponding features in Aeschylus:

Number of extant trimeters, or identifiable portions

of trimeters 74

Number of extant line joins[20] in the trimeter fragments   48

a) Interlinear hiatus, all types (cf. II 2 *b*)   11

(or 23% of the total extant line joins)

b) Interlinear hiatus, nonstop only (cf. II 2 *b*)[21] . .   4

(or 36.5% of the total of *a*, above)

c) First-foot anapaests (cf. II 3 *c*)[22]   4

d) Enjambment (cf. II 3 *d*)[23]   3

And, to complete the record:

e) Initial *rho* making position . . . . . *No instances*

(either in trimeters or other verse forms)

Obviously, great caution is required in interpreting such a
small body of evidence; and I should add that I am concerned

---

[20] By a "line join" I mean a passage where the end of one line
and the beginning of the next are preserved, *excluding* those passages where the next line is given to a different speaker.

[21] Frr. 34.3, 35.11, 171.5, 171.6.

[22] Frr. 79.1, 154, 171.3, 171.6. There is also a proper name in a
first-foot anapaest in Fr. 1 (if Kaibel's line division is correct); but
I exclude such instances from the statistics given in this volume.
Focke (p. 299) cites Frr. 24 and 172.3, only, as instances of first-foot
anapaests in Epicharmus; the first is no instance at all, the second is
a misprint for "171.3."

[23] Frr. 35.11, 171.5, 171.6.

by the fact that so high a proportion of our instances is concentrated in Fr. 171 (a notable "philosophical" fragment), even though most competent authorities seem to accept it as genuine. Still, as the evidence stands, we find in the random selection of Epicharmus' trimeters that survives an incidence of first-foot anapaests and enjambment that is slightly higher than the incidence in the *PV*, and an incidence of nonstop hiatus that is lower by only 4.5 percent.

The evidence does not allow me to go further in this direction, unless perhaps I may suggest that the liveliness and realism of the *PV*'s Prologue (difficulty *a*) might well, from what we know of Epicharman comedy, be accounted for in a similar way.

There remains difficulty (*e*), the unparalleled formal regularity observable in *PV*'s line arrangement. Enough is left of the *Unbound* to show that this concern for regularity extended beyond details to the grand design of the first two plays of the trilogy. *PV*'s female chorus from the sea was balanced in the *Unbound* by a male chorus recently delivered from the earth: Ocean seems to have been balanced by Gaia; the long prophecies to Io of a fearful journey to east and south, culminating in the African continent and in a change of fortune, were balanced by prophecies to her descendant Herakles, sweeping him westward and southward to a similar end. With this tendency to tighten up the external form, often by the simple device of symmetry, I would also associate the repetitions, especially the numerous echoes of the prologue in the *exodos*.

This feature is, I repeat, unparalleled in all Greek drama. Very faint parallels to the repetitions, the choric quatrains, and the recurrence of stichomythiae of identical length, are found in the *Oresteia* (above, Chapter II 4 *a* and Chapter II 1 *a, b*). With those slight exceptions, however, any explanation, and any justification of Aeschylean authorship, must depend on internal considerations.

In one aspect at least, the feature is characteristically Aeschylean: in its thoroughgoing *coherence*. In this monograph I have often paused to marvel at the enormous range of Aeschylus' creativity—at his flair for shaping a poem ad hoc, from minute detail up to strategic design, in total conformity with the poetic idea. No other ancient dramatist can approach him. Even when I look for his peers in this respect outside Greek literature, very few names come to mind: Dante above all; Virgil and Shakespeare, in their different ways. Now we have seen that whoever wrote the *Prometheia* insisted on symmetry, responsion and repetition at all levels of the design. I know of no Greek author who had it in him to do such a thing, with the single exception of Aeschylus. Exactly why he should have done it in this trilogy must be a matter of guesswork, unless fortune should ever restore to us the complete *Prometheia* (and, with it, the complete poetic idea). But I guess that a contributory motive, at least, may have been the mere vastness and wildness of the theme, even as we can now reconstruct it. Dante, long after, contained and articulated his cosmic subject matter by applying mathematically exact proportions to his poem, and even, to some extent, by significant repetition; I need only point to the most obvious examples, the distribution of the cantos ($1 + 3 \times 33 = 100$), and the recurrence of the word *stelle* at the end of each part. I have wondered whether Aeschylus, approaching a subject that would embrace not only the "World known to the Ancients" but their heaven too, through untold centuries of time and pain, did not instinctively regulate it by somewhat similar formal means.

Not quite all the phenomena have been accounted for. I still do not understand why *rho* should fail to make position in two passages of *PV* (above, II 2 *a*), and I know that my suggestions in explanation of the nonstop interlinear hiatus (II 2 *b*) and the regularity of arrangement (just discussed) must be counted as hypothetical. Yet the vast majority of the remaining phenomena conspire to present the same conclusion: The *Prometheus* is not radically different from the other extant Aeschylean plays; it simply develops tendencies, at all stylistic levels, that can already be traced in the "late group" of those plays. I infer that it can only have been composed by Aeschylus, and that it must be among the very latest of his works.

A summation of so much cumulative evidence is not possible. Instead, I ask leave to conclude the case by introducing the author-claimant for a few moments. Aeschylus is well on into his sixties, and in that long life he has seen and heard much; ἐκδιδάσκει πάνθ' ὁ γηράσκων χρόνος. He has known the glaring colors and the writhing monsters of the Athenian

Acropolis as it was before the Persians came. Peisistratid "tyranny" and Cleisthenic "democracy" are already faraway happenings for him, and so is the appalling humiliation—appalling even to thoughtful men among the victors—of Xerxes' pride. But those things at least conformed to a known and established pattern. Life worked much like that in the time of his father, Euphorion I, and even of his grandfather (who would have been a contemporary of Solon); in fact the continuity had not been broken, as far as one could tell, since the hero-kings reigned in Athens and Eleusis. Only the last fifteen or sixteen years of the claimant's life, from about the time of the Athenian production of the *Persae* (spring, 472) onward, have brought with them utterly unprecedented experiences. In Syracuse, where he restaged the *Persae* with great applause, he has witnessed the new-style tyranny of Hieron. In Athens, as well as in Sicily, a new and irreverent dramatic form, comedy, has firmly rooted itself. From about 468, when Sophocles first competed, the tempo has accelerated. A new tragedian and, in a sense, a new tragedy have entered the Dionysiac contest. There has been rising revolt against the political and social Establishment in Sicily after Hieron's death in 467/6, and in Athens itself from about 464/3; in both, the revolt has ended in the new-style democracy, government by free-born masses. Only the last two years, however—since the production of the *Oresteia* in spring, 458, and the claimant's last voyage to Sicily—have brought prolonged confrontation with the new-style *man*. The elderly claimant has either met or heard about the philosopher-poet-democrat Empedocles, the comedian Epicharmus or his successors in the Sicilian school, the professional rhetoricians Corax and Tisias, and the earliest sophists, such as Gorgias.

The claimant's fellow craftsman and acquaintance, Pindar, stopped his ears to all this. The claimant himself might plead guilty to having opened his—and to having composed the *Prometheia*.

The Components of the *Prometheia*

In this monograph I work on the assumption that the *PV* was part of a trilogy, called (conveniently, but without ancient authority) the *Prometheia*; and consisting of the *PV*, the *Unbound*, and the *Prometheus Pyrphoros*, in that order. I do not consider it as certain—the evidence is simply too slight for certainty—but it is the least unlikely way of accounting for the phenomena known to me. I will not here attempt to contribute yet another full-scale reconstruction of the lost plays to the stockpile, but perhaps I owe it to the reader to state as briefly as possible my reasons for this particular assumption.

   1. *Analogy.* All the evidence (collected in Pickard-Cambridge, 80–81) shows that when tragedies *connected in theme,* as opposed to monodramas, were presented on the Greek stage, they were presented in groups of three.

   2. *The "Bound" and "Unbound" were clearly composed as a unit, to be presented at one time.*[1] This is not only indicated by the titles and fragments, but also proved by

[1] This must be true whether or not Aeschylus was the author. Schmid's attempt to dissociate the two plays (attributing only the *Unbound* to Aeschylus, as a monodrama) breaks down in view of the stylistic peculiarities common to them both, not to mention the grotesque hypotheses into which Schmid himself is forced by this device.

external evidence: Schol. Med. ad *PV* 511 ἐν γὰρ τῷ ἑξῆς δράματι λύεται, cf. ad 522.

3. *The "Bound" cannot have been preceded by another play in the trilogy.* Otherwise it is impossible to see why Aeschylus should have devoted the Prologue and first two episodes almost exclusively to a careful exposition of the current situation in heaven and on earth.

4. *The third play must also have been a Prometheus play.* Of the two remaining Prometheus plays recorded in the *Catalogue,* the *Prometheus Pyrkaeus* must be excluded, since it was a satyr-play (Beazley, p. 625). There remains the *Prometheus Pyrphoros.*

5. The Medicean scholium on *PV* 94, μυριετῆ (Murray, pp. 150–151; Fr. 341 M). This runs: πολυετῆ. ἐν γὰρ τῷ Πυρφόρῳ γ′ μυριάδας φησὶ δεδέσθαι αὐτόν. The statement not only proves that the action of the *Pyrphoros* was set after the release of Prometheus[2] (and therefore could not have embraced the original theft of fire). It may well also indicate that the scholiast, who knows that the *Bound* was followed by the *Unbound* (see item 2, above), also knows that the *Pyrphoros* belonged to the same group. That would make his citation from that rare play (there are only three mentions of it anywhere, including the bare title in the *Catalogue*) more intelligible and would also give point to his anxiety to prove that there is no inconsistency here between

---

[2] Notice the perfect, δεδέσθαι. Nineteenth-century attempts to "emend" the Medicean's reading to a future were never justifiable. It may further be noted here that the Medicean is no longer our sole medieval MS source for this scholium. I find a variant of it as a gloss—still with the reading δεδέσθαι—in the manuscripts NPW (Turyn's sigla). Whether or not those manuscripts can depend directly on the Medicean scholium, it is still too early to tell.

the *Pyrphoros* and the *Bound*. For I take the drift of his note to be: "μυριετῆ must not be understood as *ten-thousand-yeared*, but as *many-yeared*; otherwise there would be a conflict with the *Pyrphoros*, where Aeschylus says that Prometheus has been bound for *three myriad* years."

6. Finally, I am not impressed by the often-stated objection that no third play is conceivable, because as far as can be seen, all the problems were solved by the end of the *Unbound*. For one thing, there is no limit to the paradoxical inventiveness of Aeschylus; witness the *Eumenides*! For another, I can no longer see solid evidence that any problems at all were solved by the end of the *Unbound*. The evidence rather suggests that the freeing of Prometheus, by Zeus's son, *against Zeus's will* (*PV* 771 ἄκοντος Διος: cf. *Unbound* Fr. 201 N=333 M, where Zeus is still ἐχθρός after the release), will simply have worse confounded the moral chaos. The only indication to the contrary is of course Fr. 202 N=334 *fin.* M, where Athenaeus remarks: "Aeschylus clearly states in the *Prometheus Unbound* that it is in Prometheus' honor that we place the garland on our head, as ἀντίποινα[3] for his chains." The inference from this etiology (Athenaeus is discussing the origin of the practice of garland-wearing) is fairly certain: at some point in the trilogy Prometheus *was* reconciled to Zeus and accepted a symbolic bond in place of the real one.[4] But the possibility might be

---

[3] A tragic word (*Pe* 476, *Eu* 268); quite possibly the actual word used by Aeschylus.

[4] The inference is of course supported by several versions of the myth that may in varying degrees be related to the Aeschylean version; especially those of Menodotos (Athenaeus 672–673). Servius on *Eclogues* 6.42 *fin.* (cf. Pliny *NH* 33.4, 37.1) and Hyginus *Astron.* 2.15.

considered that Athenaeus is here quoting from a prophecy
(e.g., by Gaia?) in the *Unbound,* which was not verified
until the last play. There are already such prophetic etiologies
in the *Bound* (732–734, 839–841).

External Grounds for Dating the *Prometheus*

The extreme chronological limits for the composition of the *PV* are the eruption of Etna in 479/8 B.C. (Marmor Parium) or *c.* 475/4 B.C. (Thucydides), evidently alluded to in *PV* 366–372, and 424 B.C., when two lines from our play were quite certainly parodied in the *Knights* (lines 758–759, 836); see Schmid (I), pp. 5 ff. This disconcertingly wide span is contracted if one accepts—as, on the whole, I do—Schmid's claim that there are echoes of the *PV*'s language in Sophocles' *Ajax* and *Antigone*. In that case the play will probably have been in existence by 441 B.C., and perhaps a few years earlier.

Within that limit, scholars who have accepted the authenticity of the *PV* have usually dated it in one of two periods, both being periods during which Aeschylus visited Sicily. Some place the play after the *Oresteia,* that is, in the period 458–456/5 B.C. The majority of German-speaking scholars, however, from Wilamowitz until the present day, prefer the period of Aeschylus' earlier Sicilian visit at the invitation of Hieron, that is, *c.* 472–468.

The reasons alleged in favor of the earlier date are almost entirely external. In fact, to accept that date one must, in my opinion, simply throw overboard or ignore the metrical and stylistic observations that have accumulated in the periodical literature of the last thirty or forty years. External evidence,

of course, is usually preferable to evidence of any other kind
in these matters. But I cannot help feeling some hesitation
as to whether the external evidence adduced here is evidence
at all.

It will be simplest to examine the case as it has been most
recently stated by Mette (I, pp. 256–257). I summarize his
reasons, and my doubts. (1) Fr. 235 N=181 M of the satyric *Sphinx* (produced with the *Septem* in spring, 467 B.C.)
is said by Mette to contain a back-reference to the *Unbound*.
His words are: "Das kann sich nur auf den 'Befreiten Prometheus' beziehen." *Nur!* To me both the meaning of the
fragment itself (quite aside from the trivial corruption),
and even more the drift of the passage of Athenaeus in
which it is preserved, seem very obscure, as they have to
others before me. All that can certainly be made out is that
Athenaeus is here contrasting (καίτοι, 'although')[1] one Aeschylean remark about Prometheus and garlands with another.
Further, such a deliberate and illusion-breaking *quotation* of
one play in another—which Mette's theory postulates—
would be unique in Aeschylus and, as far as I know, in all
extant tragedy (not omitting the satyric *Cyclops*). (2) Mette
adduces the resemblance between the fragments of Sophocles'
Triptolemos (dated, on tolerably good grounds, to 468 B.C.)
and the prophecies to Io in the *PV* as proof that the latter
play must be the earlier. But here is a whole chain of un-
certainties! The dating of the *Triptolemos* is not undisputed

---

[1] If one insisted strictly on the tenses used by Athenaeus here
(φησί · · · καίτοι εἰπών), the concessive clause would actually have
to be translated "although in the *Sphinx* he had said . . ." This
would imply that the *Sphinx* was earlier than the *Unbound*, but
I am not yet sure enough of Athenaeus' tense usage to press this
point.

(see Pearson's survey of this whole question in *The Fragments of Sophocles,* II, p. 239). Even granted that point, it is not certain that one poet is imitating the other. Both might, for instance, be modeling themselves on the "geographical" speeches of Circe to Odysseus in the *Odyssey*; and the appearance of the same metaphor, or rather poetic cliché, in *PV* 789 and *Tript.* Fr. 597 proves nothing.[2] Finally, granted that one poet is imitating the other, exactly why is it "nicht denkbar" (Mette's words) that the older poet should have imitated the younger? In my own experience of poets, a good poet who sees a good thing will take it; and let his dignity go to the devil if necessary. (3) Mette's third point is that Pindar's first Pythian, referring to a victory in summer 470 B.C., is imitated in *PV* 351–372; combining this neatly with (2), he concludes that *PV* must have been produced in March, 469 B.C. But (*a*), this suggestion assumes an uncommon rapidity of composition in Pindar combined with an uncommon haste to imitate in Aeschylus, (*b*) it is far from certain that either poet is imitating the other,[3] and (*c*) the *terminus post quem* gained in this uncertain way is only of practical use if we accept the dubious *termini ante quem* provided by Mette in (1) and (2).

[2] Are *all* the instances of the cliché "tablets of the mind" collected by Groeneboom on *PV* 789 and Pfeiffer (p. 26) supposed to be "imitations" of *PV* 789? Surely we have, rather, evidence of a *general* upsurge of Athenian public interest in reading and writing; this can also be traced, as Pfeiffer well points out, on the vase paintings (some of which date long before the *PV*, by any theory).

[3] See Zuntz (p. 59 n. 2) for arguments suggesting that both poets are inspired by a common source. A far more certain instance of Pindaric imitation occurs at *PV* 922–925 (cf. *Isthm.* 8, celebrating a victory of 478 B.C.).

BIBLIOGRAPHY

This list is primarily intended to identify the works that are mentioned by the author's name alone in the text and notes. I have also included, however, a limited number of other works bearing on the authenticity problem that I have consulted, but have not had occasion to mention. Perhaps I should explain that the appearance here of so many items under my own name is not, I hope, due to ὕβρις! My intention is just to spare myself the labor of documenting again a number of arguments that are repeated in the present work, while at the same time giving the reader the means of controlling them in detail, should he wish.

ARNOTT, P. *Greek Scenic Conventions of the Fifth Century B.C.* Oxford, 1962.
BEAZLEY, J. D. "Prometheus Fire-Lighter." *AJA* 43 (1939): 618–639.
BOCK, M. "Aischylos und Akragas." *Gymnasium* 65 (1958): 402–450.
CARLETON, S. B. B. "Interlinear Hiatus in the Tragoediae of Aeschylus." (1968; unpubl.).
CEADEL, E. B. "Resolved Feet in the Trimeters of Euripides and the Chronology of the Plays." *CQ* 35 (1941): 66–89.
CHANTRAINE, P. *Histoire du parfait grec.* Paris, 1927.
COMAN, J. *L'authenticité du Prométhée Enchaîné.* Bucharest, 1943.
DAVISON, J. A. "The Date of the Prometheia." *TAPA* 80 (1949): 66–93.

DENNISTON, J. D. *Greek Particles*. 2nd ed., revised by K. J. Dover. Oxford, 1954.

DOVER, K. J. *Lysias and the Corpus Lysiacum*. Sather Lectures, 39. Berkeley and Los Angeles, 1968.

FARNELL, L. R. "The Paradox of the Prometheus Vinctus." *JHS* 53 (1933): 40–50.

FIORI-SOLE, G. "La figura di Zeus nelle Supplici di Eschilo." *Atene e Roma* (1943): 45–56.

FOCKE, F. "Aischylos' Prometheus." *Hermes* 65 (1930): 259–304.

FRAENKEL, E. (ed.) *Aeschylus: Agamemnon.* 3 vols. Oxford, 1950.

FRIEDRICH, W. H. *Vorbild und Neugestaltung: Sechs Kapitel zur Geschichte der Tragödie.* Göttingen, 1967.

GROENEBOOM, P. *Aeschylus' Prometheus.* Groningen, 1928.

HARRISON, E. "Interlinear Hiatus in Greek Tragic Trimeters." *CR* 55 (1941): 22–25, and *CR* 57 (1943): 61–63.

HERINGTON, C. J. (I) "Aeschylus, *Prometheus Unbound*, Fr. 193." *TAPA* 92 (1961): 239–250.
(II) "A Unique Technical Feature of the *Prometheus Bound*." *CR* 13 (1963): 5–7.
(III) "Some Evidence for a Late Dating of the *Prometheus Bound*." *CR* 14 (1964): 239–240.
(IV) "Aeschylus: The Last Phase." *Arion* 4 (1965): 387–403.
(V) "The Influence of Old Comedy on Aeschylus' Later Trilogies." *TAPA* 94 (1963): 113–125.
(VI) "Aeschylus in Sicily." *JHS* 87 (1967): 74–85.

ITALIE, G. *Index Aeschyleus.* Leiden, 1955.

JENS, W. *Die Stichomythie in der frühen griechischen Tragödie.* Munich, 1955.

KAIBEL, G. *Comicorum Graecorum Fragmenta* I. Berlin, 1899.

KESELING, P. "Aischylos' Gefesselter Prometheus in Platons Protagoras und Gorgias." *PhW* (1930): 1469–1472.

KNOX, B. M. W. *The Heroic Temper.* Sather Lectures, 35. Berkeley and Los Angeles, 1964.

KÖRTE, A. "Das Prometheus-Problem." *NJA* 45 (1920): 201–213.

KRANZ, W. *Stasimon.* Berlin, 1933.

LESKY, A. *Die tragische Dichtung der Griechen.* Göttingen, 1956.

LLOYD-JONES, H. "The End of the *Seven Against Thebes.*" *CQ* 9 (1959): 80–115.

MAAS, P. *Greek Metre.* Translated by H. Lloyd-Jones. Oxford, 1962.

MÉAÚTIS, G. *L'Authenticité et la Date du Prométhée Enchaîné.* Geneva, 1960.

MEINEKE, A. *Fragmenta Comicorum Graecorum.* 5 vols. 1839–1857.

METTE, H. J. (I) *Die Fragmente der Tragödien des Aischylos.* Berlin, 1959.
(II) *Der Verlorene Aischylos.* Berlin, 1963.

NAUCK, A. *Tragicorum Graecorum Fragmenta.* 2nd ed. Leipzig, 1889.

NIEDZBALLA, F. "De Copia Verborum et Elocutione Promethei Vincti q. f. Aeschyli." Dissertation. Breslau, 1913.

OWEN, A. S. [contribution on lyric actor parts in Sophocles and Euripides in:] *Greek Poetry and Life,* pp. 149–152, Oxford, 1936.

PERETTI, A. "Osservazioni sulla lingua del Prometeo eschileo." *Stud. It. di Fil. Class.* 5 (1928).

PFEIFFER, R. *History of Classical Scholarship.* Oxford, 1968.

PICKARD-CAMBRIDGE, A. W. *The Dramatic Festivals of Athens.* 2nd ed., revised by J. Gould and D. M. Lewis. Oxford, 1968.

RIBBECK, O. *Qua Aeschylus Arte in Prometheo Fabula Diverbia Composuerit*. Berne, 1859.

RITCHIE, W. *The Authenticity of the Rhesus of Euripides*. Cambridge, 1964.

ROBERTSON, D. S. "The End of the Supplices Trilogy of Aeschylus." *CR* 28 (1924): 51–53.

RÖMER, A. "Studien zu der handschriftlichen Überlieferung des Aischylos." *Sitz-Ber. München* 2 (1888): 201–254.

ROSE, H. J. *A Commentary on the Surviving Plays of Aeschylus*. 2 vols. Amsterdam, 1957.

SCHEIN, S. L. "The Iambic Trimeter in Aeschylus and Sophocles." Dissertation. Columbia, 1967.

SCHMID, W. (I) *Untersuchungen zum Gefesselten Prometheus*. Stuttgart, 1929.
(II) "Epikritisches zum Gef. Prom." *PhW* (1931): 218–223.
(III) *Geschichte der griechischen Literatur*. I. 3 (Munich 1950): 281–308.

SKARD, E. "Ὠφελεῖν τὸν κοινὸν βίον: A remark on Prom. 613." *Symb. Osloenses* (1949): 11–18.

SMYTH, H. W. "Notes on the Anapaests of Aeschylus." *Harv. Stud.* 7 (1896): 139–165.

SNELL, B. *Scenes from Greek Drama*. Sather Lectures, 34. Berkeley and Los Angeles, 1964.

THOMSON, G. (I) (ed.) *Aeschylus, Prometheus Bound*. Cambridge, 1932.
(II) (ed.) *The Oresteia of Aeschylus*. 2nd ed. Amsterdam and Prague, 1966.

UNTERBERGER, R. *Der Gefesselte Prometheus des Aischylos*. Stuttgart, 1968.

VÜRTHEIM, J. (ed.) *Aischylos' Schutzflehende*. Amsterdam, 1928.

WACKERNAGEL, J. (I) "Sprachgeschichtliches zum Prometheus."

Verhandl. der Versamml. Deutscher Philologen 46 (1901–1902): 65.
(II) *Studien zum griechischen Perfektum.* Göttingen, 1904.

WECKLEIN, N. (I) (ed.) *Prometheus.* Translated by F. D. Allen. Boston, 1893.
(II) (ed.) *Aeschyli Fabulae.* Berlin, 1885–1893.

WENDEL, T. *Die Gesprächsanrede im griechischen Drama der Blütezeit.* Stuttgart, 1929.

WHITE, J. W. *The Verse of Greek Comedy.* London, 1912.

YORKE, E. C. (I) "Trisyllabic Feet in the Dialogue of Aeschylus." *CQ* 30 (1936): 116–119.
(II) "The Date of the Prometheus Vinctus." *CQ* 30 (1936): 153–154.

YOUNG, D. "Miltonic Light on Professor Denys Page's Homeric Theory." *Greece and Rome* 6 (1959): 96–108.

ZUNTZ, G. *The Political Plays of Euripides.* Manchester, 1955.